HOW TO BECOME A BALLOON ARTIST AND MAKE UP TO $100,000 A YEAR

An Expert's Step-By-Step Guide

by
Charles Prosper

Published by
Global Publishing Company
P.O. Box 35357
Los Angeles, CA 90035

Dedication

To Estela, without you all of this may never have happened

Acknowledgements

I am deeply indebted to the many people who were sources of inspiration, moral support, or who contributed directly to the final preparation and perfection of the manuscript. These wonderful people are: Dewann Clark of Specialized I.M.S. who did the computer typesetting, Marie Moneysmith, Bruce Wright, Mike Falcon, Yucari Lee, and Jan Cohen of *Flowers &* magazine, Elena Vinson, David Emmanuel, Josie Martin, Ron Martin, Sylvester Bland, Debra Bland, Mercedes Garcia, Darlyne Smith, Tommy Doo, Pat Thompson, Ina Rice Wilson, Fred McZeal, Clois Williams, Siggie Cohen my long-time photographer, Dorothy Gaither, Peter Parker, Star Parker, David Figueroa, Susan George, Georgeann Cooper, Susan Austin, Jene Davenport, Maria Anaya, Ligia Lopez, Carmen Bravo, Kelli Ann Clift, Margo Bouchet, Christina Deamicis, Shelia Menzies, Tonya Brown, Tiny Rilley, Jeff Buford, Akop Chichyan, Mary Bonner, Cheryl Estrada, Marla Johnson, Rebecca Williams, Doris Doakes, April Lewis, Karen Kile, Marlene Rattler, Allen Shelton, Magdalene Lawrence, Sara Ybarra, Future Henry, Jacqueline Nicholson, Jeffery Nicholson, Kathleen Touryan, Ray Trinidad, Gerald Bougham, Garnell Cooper, Charolette Cooper and Leora Legacy.

I want to sincerely thank all of these fine people, and I know they are proud of the part they have played in the realization of this work.

Cover Design and Illustrations: Charles Newton

Front Cover Photography: Yoshi Ohara Studio 6341 Yucca Street, Hollywood, California 90028

About the Author

Charles Prosper is one of the most accomplished and creative balloon artist in the nation. Starting his balloon business from an apartment living room with $500.00, he moved quickly in a few short years to open one of the most successful retail and wholesale balloon enterprises in the country. In this long awaited book, he explains the inside secrets and techniques of how <u>you</u> can become a balloon artist and make up to $100,000.00 (or more) a year.

Contents

INTRODUCTION

Little more than 10 years ago were you to suggest decorating a fancy wedding reception, a debutante ball, or a ritzy fashion show with balloons, the reaction would have been something like: "Balloons! Are you kidding? I'm not planning a children's party!" Well, this type of response is being heard less and less now because a new profession has come of age-*balloon decorating*! Now, many respected and sophisticated companies are using balloons for events where they wouldn't have even *dreamed* of doing so before. I'm talking about events like: company awards-banquets, annual Christmas parties, and even national trade show conventions for companies like Pepsi Cola, the Hyatt Hotels, Holiday Inn, Bekins, California Federal Savings, Kentucky Fried Chicken and many, many others. I know this for a fact because all of the above mentioned companies are among *my* regular accounts. In addition to decorating for many big and well-known corporations, we also do an average of 4 to 5 major wedding decorations every Saturday. My store front handles daily at least ten $30 to $40 balloon arrangements on the *slowests* of days.

With $500 saved from an unemployment check, I started my balloon gift-delivery and decoration business from an apartment, and within 2 years time while still working from this home-base, I moved quickly from an initial gross of $200 per month to a fantastic *$6000* per month! How I did this and how you can do this also is the subject of this book. To my knowledge, this book is the first and only definitive work ever to be written on what has got to be the most colorful and exciting professions to have come along in a long time.

If one were to describe the "perfect" profession as creative, fun, lucrative, beautiful, and exciting then professional balloon decorating would surely fit the bill.

Part I

THE ART AND TECHNIQUES
OF BALLOON DECORATING

Chapter One
THE HISTORY OF
BALLOON DECORATING

The history of professional balloon decorating has been relatively brief but utterly fascinating as it has become almost an overnight phenomenon.

Joe Del Vecchio

The age of the balloon started in year 1976 when Joe Del Vecchio brain-stormed a concept that before this time would have probably been laughed back into non-existence. Mr. Del Vecchio thought, "People have been sending flowers for years as expressions of love, thanks, well-wishes, and friendship. And of course balloons have always had the inexplicable power to bring a smile to our faces, to bring out innocence, love, joy, and happiness that is the child within all of us. What better and more effective gesture of caring could there be than to send someone a bouquet of balloons instead of flowers." Hence he came up with the concept of the *balloon bouquet*, and started Balloon Bouquets, Inc. in Washington. So much success did Mr. Del Vecchio have with his idea that in 1976 the company opened branches in 14 cities across the country making Balloon Bouquets, Inc. the first nation-wide balloon delivery service. The first balloon bouquets were done by inflating 2 dozen nine or eleven inch latex balloons with helium (the gas which makes all balloons float) in a rainbow of colors and tying to the ends of each balloon a matching-color ribbon. They were then bunched and tied together and were delivered as a concept of "instead of flowers, send balloons." The balloon bouquet delivery service was promoted initially to celebrities and upper income clients who responded quite readily to this novel idea. For a long time it was believed that middle and lower income groups were not the markets for such an avant-garde concept. But 1 year after I started my career as a balloon artist, I found that this upper-income-group-only acceptance ideas was very, very, wrong. I found out very quickly that *everybody* loves a balloon and everybody has the *need* to celebrate. Is it not that when we *celebrate* life that we truly, truly *experience* it?

Balloons Bouquets, Inc. coined the word *balloon bouquet* and have recently obtained the *exclusive* rights to use this phrase as part of their trademark. In all of your promotions and advertising, you should say balloon *arrangement* and never *"balloon bouquet"*.

Treb Heining

There are some balloon enthusiasts particularly those few who have been around since the early days here in Los Angeles who will almost bow their heads and genuflect if someone only *mentions* the name Treb Heining. Who *is* Treb Heining? Well, for all practical purposes, it might be said that Treb Heining, better known as Treb, is the father of professional balloon art decorating. He was the first person to come up with the concept of the spiral weave balloon arch (also around 1976). Treb was the innovator of the now widely used paper-clip technique for holding the balloons together in sections (called helixes) that are placed one-by-one onto an outstretched cord and like pearls onto a necklace, bunched together, then woven one section after another into a spiraling swirl of color. (More on the how-to of doing the spiral weave arch in later chapters). Treb is also credited for orchestrating some of the largest balloon decorating jobs when balloon artistry was still an infant industry. Such grand scale jobs were: doing Disneyland's 30th anniversary celebration, the world's largest birthday cake out of balloons, the first vertical-floating balloon American flag, and many other spectacular and breath-taking balloon decoration accomplishments. He was the first to demonstrate to the world that balloons could not only be a viable art form but a real and lucrative industry. Treb is known to command as much as $100,000 on a single decoration contract. We thank him for his contributions as pioneer in one of the greatest industries to have come along in centuries.

Balloons By Prosper

Writing this section I guess, is somewhat like writing a congradulatory letter to oneself. Nevertheless a story worth telling is told none the better than by the one who experienced it. This is my success story.

Back in 1980, I was working as a Spanish by-lingual alcohol counselor. (I majored in foreign languages when I studied at the University of New Orleans and subsequently became very fluent in Spanish and French). The counseling program where I was employed lost its funding and there were massive lay-offs throughout the agency. A co-worker friend of mine laughed and said, "Well, Charles,

I'll see you in the unemployment line." I blurted out, "Look, if I have to stand on a street corner with a visor cap and a coin purse and sell balloons, I'll do it." After a night's rest this idea didn't seem so absurd to me. So with my last $200 I had left in my savings account, I went out and bought a small helium tank, a spool of string, balloons and went out to sell in the annual Hollywood Christmas Parade. To my delight and amazement, I sold $100 that night. Following that night, I took to the parks and street corners, but most days I only made from $30 to $35 a day and many other days I was chased from the streets by the Los Angeles police because there are ordinances which don't allow vending on public corners. I soon received notice from my landlord to pay my past-due rent or *get out*. It was then that I decided to quickly seek "regular" employment again. I landed a job working as a waiter from 4:00 A.M. to 11:00 A.M. in the morning and continued my vending efforts in the evenings. Another parade was scheduled during the Christmas holiday season. It was very, very cold that night and I think I must have made no more than $15 for my entire night's effort. My feelings began to run very, very low as I, in a moment of despondency, released all of the remaining balloons into the air. "Here I am," I said to myself, "a college graduate standing on a street corner selling balloons. If mom only could see me now." Then the question of all great turning points came into my mind: "There *must* be a better way." Inexplicably a new surge of *determination* coursed through my being. I went home and got a good night's sleep.

The next day as I was eating a double dip cone of cherry vanilla ice cream at Baskin Robbins after getting off from my morning waiter's job, I noticed a small ad in one of those free community newspapers. Someone was advertising a service of bunches of balloons *delivered* for parties and special occasions. "Wow! "I said to myself," now that's a novel approach!" I called the phone number listed, and it was of a lady who'd recently started this interesting business from home. I immediately ordered her 2 dozen arrangement which she sold for $24.00. When I received this cluster of rainbow balloons, I was impressed that instead of ordinary string, she used matching curling ribbon. I asked where she advertised and she told me in *Los Angeles Magazine's* classified (read by all of the celebrities and upper income group of Los Angeles.) It was to my great surprise that I found *other* small balloon delivery operations as well including a very large ad of Balloon Bouquets of Southern California who claimed also to have an *album* of balloon decorations. "How interesting," I thought.

When I went in to see this decoration album, it was there that I saw for the first time a balloon arch. I was utterly fascinated. "This *is* the better way!" I thought. As I looked around, I noticed that the bags of balloons (called grosses) that were stacked on the shelves carried the label Qualatex which I later discovered to be the finest quality of balloons in the world. While talking to the person in charge, I heard with great enthusiasm the mention of the name Treb for the first time. Upon leaving out of that store on that eventful day, my mind was racing with ideas at the speed of light thinking of all of the creative possibilities that I knew that I could achieve with this new approach. I had learned after asking numerous questions that certain plastic discs were used for forming single arch techniques and that the spiral balloon weaves were done by tying the balloons around an outstretched fish line. Upon arriving home I began to experiment. Through trial-and-error, I achieved my first single arch and weave arch. I then had an artist friend of mine sketch out my balloon arch designs with multi-color markers. Immediately I saw great potential for this combination balloon delivery and balloon decoration business.

Having decided to build a home-base business, I realized that I would need capital to promote it. To get enough starting capital to be able to go at it full-force, I also took an *evening* waiter's job that scheduled from 3:00 P.M. To 12 midnight *along with* my 4:00 A.M. to 11:00 A.M. shift. I was sleeping around 3 hours per night, but I had decided to do this for at least two years while building up my business and savings. Instead of taking my hour to eat lunch in the employees cafeteria, I would eat while I worked and use my precious lunch hour to design decoration concepts and to promote my balloon arrangement delivery services to my co-workers. For a year, I managed to average one $200 wedding decoration per month and about one or two $28 balloon arrangement deliveries per week. But this routine after a year was more rigorous than I had thought and I was "burning out". It was about this time when a complete physical breakdown was almost imminent, but good fortune smiled a super-helper in my path -Estela Pulido- my friend and partner who is responsible for helping me build Balloons By Prosper to its present level of nation-wide prominence.

We met while she was studying a career of cosmetology, and I remember well that day in the restaurant when I showed her my early photos of my rainbow arch tunnel designs, my wedding concepts, and my balloon arrangements. I think I had about 4 color photos at the time. She practically jumped out of her seat with excitement. "This is simply *beautiful*!" she said. "I've never seen anything like this in my life. Lend me these photos and I am sure that I can sell these balloon arrangements at my cosmetology school." And sell she did. Estela was selling an average of three $28 balloon arrangements everyday for almost 3 weeks. I was almost speechless. It was one evening that she looked me straight into the eye and said, "Charles, why keep burning yourself out with those nickel and dime waiter jobs? Quit them both, and *concentrate* on your balloon decoration business. I've decided to quit studying cosmetology to help you. If need be, I'll work as a maid cleaning houses to help you with any emergency expenses. Charles, you have a lot of creative talent. Go for it!" Upon hearing those words, I could hear the musical score of the movie *Rocky* playing triumphantly in the background.

I quit both jobs immediately and I began to concentrate on new designs and new ways of promoting my born-again business. Every morning at 6:00 A.M., I would brainstorm for 1 hour, with pencil and paper in hand, new and creative ways to promote Balloons By Prosper. One of my most notable ideas, was the day I decided to get a copy of the California Business Magazine annual issue, listing the top 100 California corporations. Since this was in the month of November, I systematically called each company and asked the person answering the phone: "Who is the person who would probably be in charge of the decoration aspect of your employees Christmas party?" I would hear responses such as, "I'm glad you called; you just relieved me of a lot of hassle." During these promotions, I sold an average of $500 per day in decorations for 2 consecutive weeks! And today companies like Kentucky Fried Chicken. Bekins Movers, Pepsi Cola, California Federal Savings, The Hyatt and Holiday Inn Hotel chains are still my clients. During one of my brainstorming sessions, I decided to specialize in weddings. I would contact *small*-operation caterers, wedding photographers, dee jays, and wedding cake decorators. I offered them 10% off the top of whatever their referrals spent on decorations. I would make this offer to *everybody*. I recommend that you work with *small* operations first because these home-based business persons are more plentiful and are more willing to send you their clients on a regular basis than the bigger operations. It was during this time that I discovered that minorities especially blacks and Hispanics were rapidly becoming my best clients. One reason for this was that until I came along, professional balloon decorating on a grand scale had *never* been done in these communities. I'd leave business cards on all of the tables right in between the salt and pepper shakers at all of the wedding decorations we did. The result was 2 *new* wedding jobs for every wedding we did. Working from an apartment as my business base, I began to average 3 to 4 major wedding decorations a week, averaging $300 each. As Estela continued to learn and practice decoration techniques, there was something very interesting I noticed about her. Her hands. The speed at which she was able to do all of the most complicated weave techniques was phenomenal. When I saw her one day call out instructions to a crew of our part-time workers while twisting and placing the weave into place *with one hand*, I knew I had found a winner. (It was Estela who later discovered and mastered the technique of doing numbers and letters without using any internal supportive structures such as wire framing or PVC. More on this in Chapter 9, Doing Numbers-Without PVC.)

Within 2 short years, I outgrew my apartment and opened up a storefront whereupon Balloons by Prosper's reputation soared to level of nationwide prominence. Our unique concepts and designs such as our Bride and Groom, Snowmen, Poinsettia Flowers, Christmas Wreath, Balloon Clowns, Balloon Fruit, and many others have appeared in national magazines throughout the country.

Professional balloon decorating is still an infant industry and there is indeed room for more balloon artists who are destined to leave their mark in the annals of its history.

Welcome to the world of professional balloon decorating.

Chapter Two
SELECTING YOUR BALLOONS, TANKS, AND ACCESSORIES

The basic tools of the balloon artist are: balloons (of course), helium, and accessories such as ribbon, plastic discs, paper clips, fish line, twine, and bricks. We will take a look at each of these essential tools one-by-one, starting with:

Selecting Your Balloons

Contrary to popular opinion of the general public, all balloons are *not* alike and there are indeed different qualities and brands of balloons available to the balloon artist. When it comes to the selection of latex rubber balloons, I am very dogmatic-*Qualatex*. These balloons are put out by the Pioneer Balloon Company of Witchita, Kansas and are the *best*. I have tried many, many brands of balloons in my 8 year career as a balloon artist, but no balloon company comes even close to the variety, quality, sheen, and selection of the Qualatex brand balloon. At the balloon artist's disposal, Qualatex balloons offer more than 25 essential colors and a variety of necessary balloon sizes. The 25 essential colors as I teach them are divided into the 4 basic categories:

Standard	*Jewel Tone*	*Fashion Tone*	*Metallic*
Dark Green	Ruby Red	Wintergreen	Gold
Yellow	Emerald Green	Spring Lilac	Silver
Orange	Sapphire Blue	Desert Turquoise	
Pink	Citrine Yellow	Georgia Peach	
Pale Blue	Amethyst Violet	Ivory Sand	
White	Diamond Clear	Hot Rose	
	Quartz Purple	Golden Rod	
	Crystal Brown		
	Garnet Wine		
	Onyx Black		

There is also a red and dark blue under the standard color category, but I find the *ruby* red and *sapphire* blue far superior in terms of sheen and richness of color. When I explain the Art of Color Combinations in Chapter 7, I will be referring to colors in all of these 4 categories.

Qualatex balloons are sold in bags called *grosses* of 144 balloons per gross. The essential balloon sizes which I teach are the 5", 9", 11", and 16". There are larger and smaller sizes than these like the 40" and 4" sizes, but for most practical purposes the 5", 9", 11", and 16" sizes are all you'll really need. A gross of 5" will cost you about $4.00, 9" about $6.00, 11" about $8.00, and 16" about $17.00 depending on the balloon category. Jewel tones usually cost a couple dollars more per gross than standard colors. Metallic gold and silver are usually slightly higher than the jewel tones.

You cannot buy direct from the Pioneer Balloon Company, but rather and more conveniently you can buy your needed Qualatex balloons from any one of their master distributors throughout the country located in your area. To find out who the closest Qualatex master distributor in your area call or write:

Pioneer Balloon Company
555 N. Woodlawn Avenue
Witchita, Kansas 67208
(316) 685-2266

There is another kind of balloon also widely used by florists and balloon enthusiasts which is a silvery foil looking balloon made out of polyester material popularly called the *mylar*. Mylars are used mostly in balloon arrangement gift deliveries and because they are usually printed with a variety of messages and cartoon characters, they cannot be an effective and esthetic means of balloon artistry. Mylars are not to be confused with the Qualatex metallic gold and silver colors which are *latex* material.

Although I have extolled the virtues of the Pioneer brand *latex* balloon, there are many quality *mylar balloon companies*. Such are: Anagram International of Minneapolis, Minnesota; Flowers, Inc. Balloons; Amerilloons, and many, many more. Most master distributors of Qualatex latex balloons will usually carry a wide variety of popular mylar brand names and designs as well. Mylars come in a variety of sizes from the very small mini mylars of 4" to the super-large 36". The most popular size however, is the 18" mylar which will sell wholesale any where from .60 to $1.00 and can be sold retail from $2.00 to $4.00 each.

The Helium Tank

That magic gas which gives latex and mylar balloons alike its lift is called *helium*. Helium is a colorless and odorless gas obtained from the earth which by being lighter than air causes balloons to float. It is non-toxic and non-flammable, but it is not recommended to be inhaled as some people playfully do causing their vocal cords to momentarily constrict allowing them the noble honor to be able to talk like Donald Duck for a fleeting few seconds. A super big gulp of this gas can cause suffocation and a surprised victim gasping for breath.

Helium was discovered in 1868 in the atmosphere during a solar eclipse by French astronomer Pierre Janssen, and the gas was first isolated from terrestrial sources in 1895. In the early 20th century, helium was still a laboratory curiosity. Commercial production of helium did not begin until 1918 by Airco Industrial Gases and then the helium filled balloon was confined to circuses, carnivals, and recreation parks. The balloon decoration boom did not start until 1976 with the advent of Balloon Bouquets, Inc. (See Chapter 1). The Silver Satellite mylar by CTI, Inc. in 1977 was the *first* mylar.

When filled, a latex balloon will last anywhere from 5 hours to 24 hours depending on the size and quality of the balloon. An 11" Qualatex balloon will last about 24 hours if they are tied properly. Most mylar balloons are heat sealed with a special mylar heat sealing machine which you can obtain from your distributor or by a woman's curling iron. They will last inflated from 2 to 4 weeks if sealed properly. Helium is compressed in large metal cylinders, the most common size being 245 cubic feet. This size cylinder will hold roughly 500 11" helium filled balloons. This size cylinder weighs around 137 lbs, so a small hand truck and chain is necessary to move it about safely. Most balloon distributors will also rent helium tanks. Depending on where you go, you may pay anywhere from $30 to $60 per tank to rent. Some places will charge you from $50 to $150 returnable deposit on *each* tank. In some cases depending on your credit standing or negotiating ability, you may get a waiver on the deposit. The time will also vary in the length some places will allow you to keep their tanks. It can vary from 3 to 30 days. I sometimes go through 30 tanks a month, and in some months many more, but I have established very good relations with my suppliers. I pay as little as $30 per tank, with no deposit, get free delivery, and can keep my tanks more than a month if I need to. So as you can see in terms of getting tanks, it pays to shop around. But no matter where you go, you should always be able to make a high profit margin when you sell your decorations. A $40 tank of 500 eleven inch helium filled balloons should gross you at least $500 worth of business if you have the right designs and if you know how to price them properly.

To be able to use a helium tank professionally, you need a properly equipped helium tank *valve*. A properly equipped valve has the following features: a gauge, a vertical push valve tip, disc pin for doing single arches, built in razor for cutting ribbon, and is preferably of the wrenchless variety which can tightly be secured by hand.

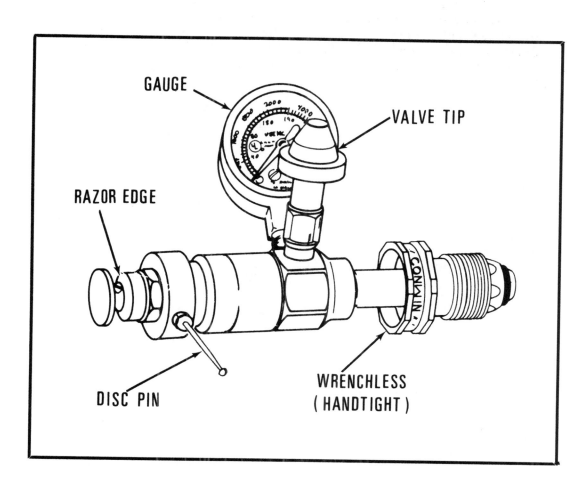

GAUGE

VALVE TIP

RAZOR EDGE

CONLIN

DISC PIN

WRENCHLESS
(HANDTIGHT)

The Helium Valve

Though there are many less expensive valves without gauges that can just as easily fill up your balloons, make no mistake about it, a gauge is a *very* important feature. This reminds me of the day many years ago when I went out to do one of my first major wedding decorations. There I was, all excited about doing a spectacular 6 arch tunnel design over a dance area. Suddenly while doing the 5th arch, I heard a very faint hissing sound coming out of my valve. I was out of helium! By not having a gauge, I had no idea as to where I stood to be able to finish. Luckily there was still some helium left in another tank I'd left at home. I rushed home and made it back in time to finish the decoration. (And for those of you who think that you absolutely must have a van or station wagon to start - *not so!*) I operated for years by lying my helium tank in the back seat of my 1972 Plymouth Valiant, placing my hand cart in the trunk and did just fine. Where there's a will, there's a way.

When a 245 cubic foot helium cylinder is full, it will read 2500 PSI, and as it empties, the gauge needle will eventually indicate 2000, 1500, 1000, and then hit a small metal point at zero. The black notches that you see in between each of the basic PSI measurements just mentioned can be used to get a rough count of how many balloons you have left in your tank. Let's say that the needle on your gauge is at 1500 PSI. You simply start at that point and count 20 balloons for every black notch you touch as you move down toward the zero point. You would read it like 20,40,60,80,100,120 balloons counting in jumps of twenties until you hit the zero point.

Most helium valves (sometimes called helium regulators) have only one valve tip. However Conwin Carbonic Co. of Los Angeles, California has come up with a marvelous *3 valve regulator*! This means that instead of 2 or 3 workers all crowded around *one* valve tip, they can each *simultaneously* inflate, tie, and cut having only one tank. Using a *single* valve and 3 workers used to take us about 15 minutes to do a 50-balloon arch. With a 3 valve regulator, we do it in *3 minutes*! Reduced decoration time means more decorations that you can program in a day. And more decorations done means more money earned. Conwin Carbonic Co. aside from being a Qualatex master distributor, manufacturers a variety of valves including their deluxe 3-way valve. I suggest that you obtain both a single tip valve with gauge, disc pin, cutter blade, as well as ordering from Conwin Carbonic, Co. their 3-way valve. A single-tip valve with all the necessary features will cost about $50 in most places. Conwin Carbonic's 3-way valve is about $85.(Be sure to request a gauge attached). You may request their catalogue and order from them UPS by calling or writing:

Conwin Carbonic Co.
4510 Sperry Street
Los Angeles, California 90039
(213) 245-2842

Upon emptying a helium cylinder, replace the metal cap and tie a ribbon around the neck. This is your way of knowing which tanks are empty and which tanks have helium. If there is still helium in a tank after finishing a job, do a balloon count as was explained above and mark the tank by writing the remaining number onto the back of one of your business cards and tape it onto the side the tank.

If you really take your decorating seriously, you may purchase from your wholesale distributors a very attractive cloth cylinder covers made out of durable machine washable fabric that come in bright colors of red, royal blue, yellow, and forest green. You might even want to buy one to see how it is constructed then have a seamstress do custom made cylinder covers for you with material that has your *logo* printed on it. Check in your city's yellow pages under seamstress or custom uniforms. Helium cylinders can get very rusty around the bottom and on the sides depending on how well it was stored by the person who rented it before you. Most of the places you'll decorate on a large scale will probably be in very elegant settings. Who wants to see a cruddy tank creating an eyesore while you work?

Your Accessories

The principal accessories of the balloon artist are 3/16" ribbon, plastic discs, paper clips, fish line, twine, bricks, scissors, and transparent tape.

There are basically two types of ribbon that should be a part of your decoration equipment. These are: 3/16" curling ribbon and 3/16" mylar ribbon. Curling ribbon comes in spools of 500 yards and is available in colors: white, silver, pastel pink, hot pink, cerise, rose, red, burgundy, peach, orange, gold, yellow, nile green, emerald, pastel blue, turquoise, royal blue, lilac, purple, brown, and black. The principle behind using the colored curling ribbon for decorating is that if you have a red balloon, you must us a red ribbon with it, or if you have a yellow balloon, than a yellow ribbon must be attached to it, a lilac balloon-a lilac ribbon, and so on and so forth. The idea is that visually the color flows from the balloon and extends downward and into the ribbon. The silver mylar ribbon is best used as "ceiling cascades" whenever permissible by attaching them to helium filled balloons and covering as much of a ceiling as possible creating a silvery cascade effect. Curling ribbon and mylar ribbon can usually be obtained from your Qualatex wholesale distributors. This type of ribbon is easily found because florist are using it a great deal also with their balloon-flower arrangements. For easy access and storage, ribbon racks that hold up to 20 spools are also available.

A spool of 3/16" curling ribbon of 500 yards will usually go for about $2.00 a spool, and 3/16" mylar ribbon is about $6.00 a spool.

Plastic discs are another very important piece of equipment to the balloon artist. This is another item which most wholesale distributors will carry. The plastic disc is a flat round-shaped clear plastic disc of about 1/2" in diameter with a small hole in the middle through which the ends of latex balloons are pushed by means of the disc pin which is part of your helium valve. This is an essential technique for doing the single balloon arch which is explained at length in Chapter 5-The Single Arch.

The paper clip tie-technique is the innovation of Treb Heining and is now widely used and the standard technique for doing the spectacular spiral balloon weave designs explained thoroughly in Chapter 6-The Weave. Fish line is also widely used for doing *large* weave arches, but I strongly advise against it. Fish line, even if you use 40 to 60 lb strengths to do a weave, being plastic, has a tendency to stretch and stretch just like taffy. Every time you push a balloon helix or section into place there is a risk that just as you are midway -snap- your weave breaks. Now, you must tie it back at a very weak point that is very likely to snap again in the same place. Do to the speed and forcefullness at which you should work, a much better material for strength and resistance is natural *twine*. I speak from experience. I can remember the day we did our first large decoration on the outside. It was a giant "97" to celebrate the city of Compton, California's 97th anniversary. There we were, five of us, at 4:00 a.m. in the morning doing a giant "97" in balloons for 9:00 a.m. It was very windy that morning, and we had to work quickly because we were new at this. This was a learn by doing experience. We must have spent 2 hours to finish just the "9" which we anchored to the ground with a large concrete block. Suddenly, there was a violent gust of wind, and like an angry marlin writhing to free itself, the number "9" whipped back and snapped, soaring into the air before anyone had time to react. I shouted, "We've got to do it again!" So, then with 2 hours of experience under our belts, we finished it the *second* time in 1 hour flat. Thanks to the benevolence of God, both the "9" and the "7" held up until the event was over later in the afternoon. We had received a crash course on the drawbacks of fish line. There is however a place for the use of fish line for the balloon artist. It is in doing inside wall techniques of letters and numbers, using *5" air inflated balloons*. More about this fascinating technique for doing letters, names, and numbers in Chapter 9.

Regular concrete bricks wrapped in foil paper serve as weights or bases for both single arches and spiral weaves. More to come on the Single Arch and Weave in late chapters.

Scissors and transparent tape conclude the list of basic materials that you will need and use for doing the special balloon arrangements for table centerpieces that you will learn in Chapter 4-The Balloon Arrangement.

Chapter Three
THE 7 DON'TS OF
BALLOON DECORATING

In this chapter, I will go into the 7 most common mistakes made by beginning balloon decorators. These 7 most common mistakes, I call the *7 dont's of balloon decorating* which are:

1. Don't mix-match ribbon and balloons.

2. Don't use printed balloons.

3. Don't use message or cartoon mylars.

4. Don't do single arches or bouquets on the outside.

5. Don't leave doors open while you're decorating.

6. Don't leave your balloons in the path of direct air-conditioning.

7. Don't over-inflate balloons.

Let's take a look at these 7 don'ts one-by-one:

1. *Don't mix-match ribbon and balloons*-One of the basic principles of effective decorating is to know how to create color flow from balloon to ribbon. A purple balloon means a purple ribbon attached and a pink balloon means a pink ribbon attached. The only exception to this rule is in the case of silver mylar ribbon which is neutral and suitable to attach to any color balloon.

2. *Don't use printed balloons*-What you are learning to do is a true *art* form. Would you imprint "Happy Birthday" across a Picasso painting, if you could afford to give someone such a prestigious gift? Of course, you wouldn't. Nor should you even *dream* of letting your clients talk you into printing their names or special messages onto your balloon works of art. For one thing, if it is a true piece of balloon artistry, you will have to stand back at least 10 or 20 feet to appreciate it. And at that distance, your eye really can't read anything. The eye is trying to behold the work of art and at the same time is distracted by some scribble all over the balloons' surface that looks from a distance no more than unintended *grafitti*.

3. *Don't use message or cartoon mylars*-Even worse than latex printed balloons to do weaves or single arches is the use of message or cartoon mylar balloons. Never use this type of balloon with an elegant centerpiece arrangement that you might do at a wedding.

4. *Don't do single arches or single balloons on the outside*-Doing single arches or balloon cluster centerpiece arrangements on the outside can spell only one thing-*disaster*-because once you are on the outside, you are no longer in a controlled environment. You are at the mercy of wind, heat, sun, and maybe even rain. Single arches and balloon centerpiece arrangements on the outside, unlike the weave, do not resist strong gusty winds very well. Once while decorating a windy patio and pool party, the balloon arrangement on one of the guest tables beat one guy so much in the face that he grabbed the balloons in anger and let them go into the air. On another occassion, Estela and I were decorating the outside driveway and entrance of the Hyatt Hotel with 6 single arches which traversed from one side of the entrance-driveway to the other forming an arch tunnel of the entrance. Everything went fine until wind and rain started to blow, and the cars

started to enter. The wind blew the arches all the way to the asphalt floor and all of the fancy Mercedes and Rolls Royces came in ripping all of our work to shreds. They allowed us, however, to do them all over on the inside, but boy did we really learn our lesson.

5. *Don't leave doors open while you're decorating*-When you allow latex balloons to be exposed to draft, direct sun, or glare, within a very short time, they start to become opaque, whittish, and ashy looking. They start to lose all of their fresh, original sheen. Of course, your client or any *inexperienced* eye may not even notice this change, but as a professional you *must* be aware of this. In the case of diamond clear or transparent balloons opaquing of *this* balloon is quickly noticeable.

6. *Don't leave your balloons in the path of direct air-conditioning*-The same effect that an open-door draft will have on the sheen of your balloons is the effect of direct air-conditioning. If you leave an arrangement of clear balloons in the path of direct air-conditioning, within 30 minutes you will have milky looking opaque balloons. Avoid the path of direct air-conditioning.

7. *Don't over-inflate balloons*-I think that this is the cardinal crime of most would-be balloon artists. The art of balloon decorating is achieved by slightly under inflating the balloons and carefully maintaining each balloon the exact same size as the rest.

Chapter Four

THE BALLOON ARRANGEMENT

In looking at the balloon arrangement, we will be basically looking at two major categories: a) gift deliveries and b) table centerpiece arrangements.

Gift Deliveries

Doing gift deliveries is probably the easiest way to get started doing balloons. A gift delivery is not really a "decoration". Many of the basic rules of large-scale hall decorating are side-stepped. The idea of the balloon cluster gift delivery is to provide persons with a means of sending an interesting and colorful gift idea for birthdays, anniversaries,"get wells", "I love you's", and "what-nots". The easiest balloon arrangement to do which you can deliver by just stuffing them in the back seat of any medium-sized car is the original 2 dozen multi-color rainbow cluster which you can sell from $24 to $28. This arrangement is comprised of 2 dozen 11" *hand*-tied helium filled balloons with matching curling ribbon. Now, I stress that you must use *11" balloons* only and *hand*-tie a knot at the tip after you fill them. Eleven inch balloons will last maybe 8 hours longer than 9" balloons. When you hand-tie your knot, this will also give additional hours of floating life to your balloons more than if you were to use plastic discs and attach them to the ribbon using a disc-tyer. (*Plastic discs should be used for doing single arches only.*)

To do a balloon properly, you inflate an 11" balloon, being careful not to *over*-inflate it into a huge pear shape. Over-inflation aside from its lack of aesthetics causes extreme tension inside the balloon allowing many to start spontaneously popping when you are transporting them from one place to another. Tie your knot. Then get roughly a 6 foot length of a matching curling ribbon, loosely tie a simple over-hand knot and place it over and *behind* the balloon knot. Be sure you place the ribbon *behind* the balloon knot. Then simply tie a bow like you were tying a shoe and you have your first of your 2 dozen balloon arrangement.

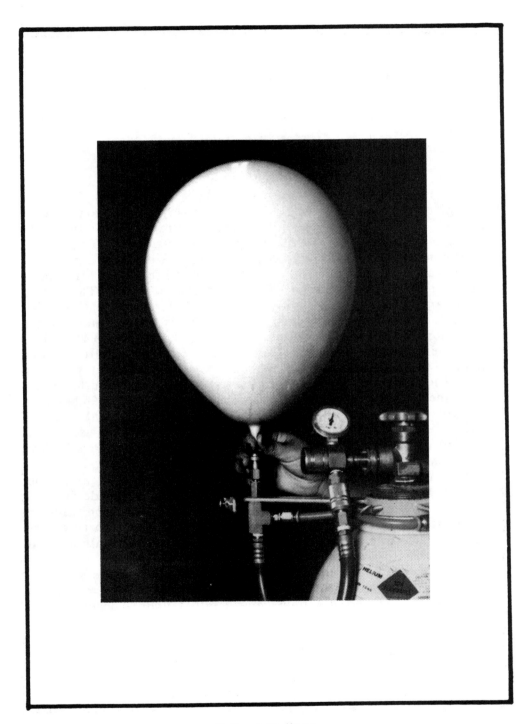

Tying A Balloon
Step 1

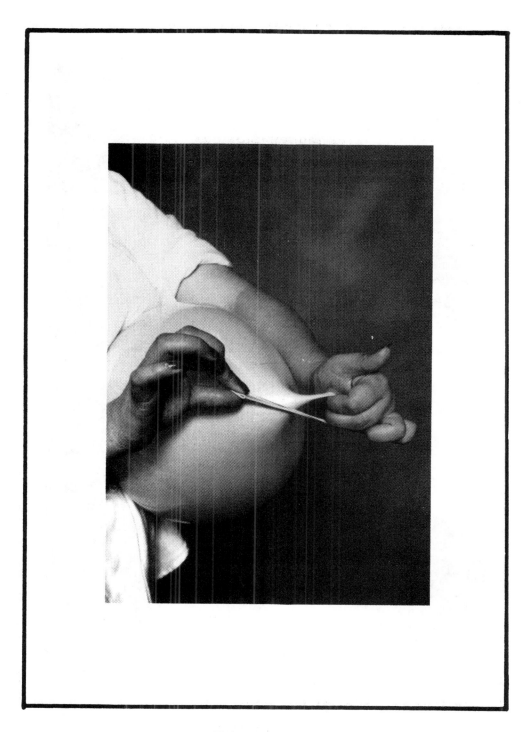

Tying a Balloon
Step 2

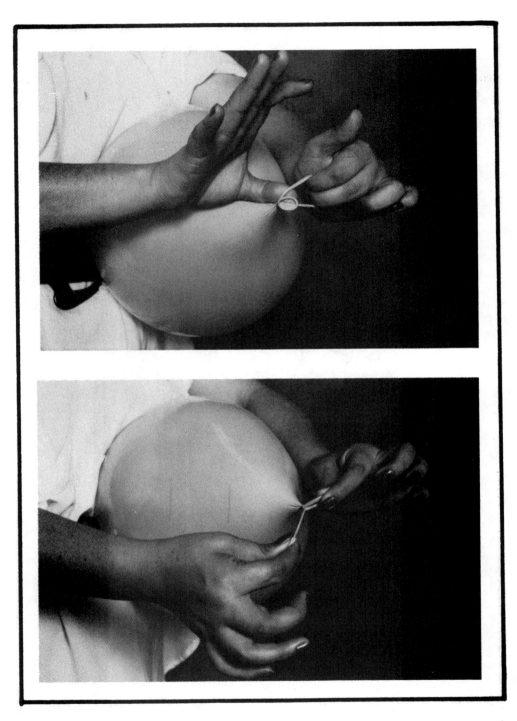

Tying A Balloon
Step 3

28

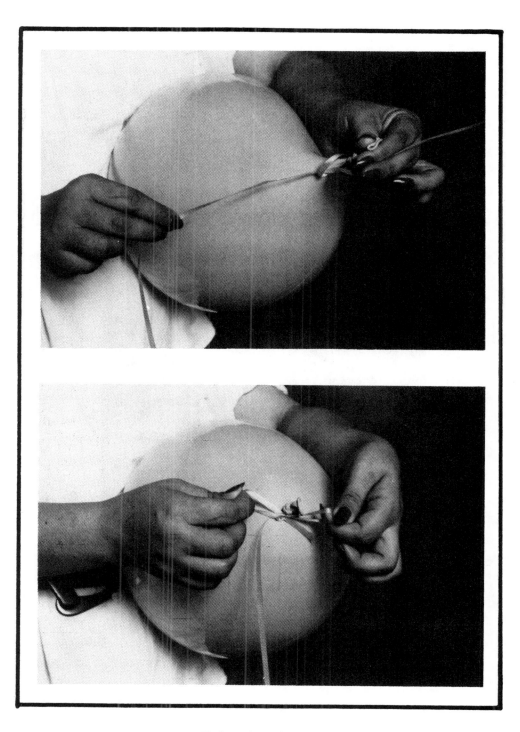

**Tying A Balloon
Step 4**

Tying A Balloon
Step 5

When you have done all 2 dozen in this fashion, it is always a good idea to throw in a couple of extra balloons without saying anything. If one or two balloons should pop along the way you will still be able to deliver your promised 2 dozen. If none pop along the way, the customer receives *two extra balloons.* They usually won't say anything to you, but they will usually call you again because they just love it when they think you can't count where it winds up in their favor. After inflating and tying ribbon to each of your 2 dozen balloons have someone hold them all in one bunch and tie a 1 foot piece of ribbon (any color) around the arrangement to keep them together. You tie this piece of ribbon around your balloons by tying a simple over hand knot and then a bow much like you tied the ribbon to each individual balloon. When transporting them, grab your balloon as high up to the neck of the arrangement as possible. This allows your more control over any windy surprises on the outside. Push them in the back seat of your car. (You may need a little help getting them in. Getting them out is much easier.)

In my early days, I would dress up in an eye-catching delivery outfit of white shoes, maroon pants, white long-sleeve shirt, a maroon bow tie and white gloves. To boot, I would *sing* a special happy birthday tune that my brother Bernard penned. I was an instant attraction everytime I went out. For every singing telegram balloon cluster delivered, I would come home and find at least 2 more orders waiting for me on my telephone answering machine. And, mind you, I am no singer not even by a long shot, but *anybody* can hold a happy birthday tune. If you really like this approach, you can start an entertainment-like service, hiring part-time performers as independent contractor celebrity look-alikes and have them go out to sing and deliver your arrangement. For these type of services, you can easily charge $60 to $100 for a 5 minute performance. You can dress up in a white gorilla suit with your balloons and build a very nice business for yourself. When Michael Jackson and his Thriller album was at the top of the charts, I used to have a high school student who was a very good performer and Michael Jackson look-alike. I charged $75 for a 1 dozen balloon delivery and 5 minute performance. He kept $25. While things were going good, we had the time of our lives with this act.

If you like the delivery-entertainment approach, it's a good idea to bring along a good cassette player with music so you can lip sync if you don't happen to be a professional singer. And how many of us are?

A successful 2 dozen rainbow balloon arrangement would contain:

```
    3 ruby  red
    2 orange
    2 citrine yellow
    2 dark green
    2 sapphire blue
    2 quartz purple
    2 pink
    2 pale blue
    2 spring lilac
    2 metallic silver (mylar ribbon)
 +  3 diamond clear (any color ribbon)
   24 Qualatex brand balloons
```

(See Chapter 2.)

Be sure to always attach one of your business cards to the arrangement by simply punching a hole toward the end of the card and tying it onto the ribbon that's holding your balloons together. You may ask your customer if he or she would like to send a short message along with it which you may write on the back of the business card that you attach. When it comes to writing down personal messages for clients, be very professional. No matter how intimate it is, just write it down in an unimpressed, matter-of-fact way.

The first balloon cluster gift deliveries to go around were the 2 dozen helium filled deliveries. This, however, as might be expected, has improved and the balloon arrangement gift deliveries are becoming more and more sophisticated. One major drawback of a 2 dozen balloon delivery is that if it is delivered to an office situation it can easily over-power a secretary's desk if she happens to be the recipient. Estela, my partner, has recently designed some new balloon arrangement ideas that have been selling like wildfire. They are smaller arrangements, more artistic, and include an additional gift along with the balloons. The gifts can be kept long after the balloons themselves have gone down. Examples of some of these new and highly successful concepts use stuffed animals like white poodles or teddy bears that are placed on handmade cardboard platforms wrapped in a silver or gold foil. The platform and stuffed animal are wrapped in clear cellophane and a big attractive bow is tied on the top onto which are attached a half dozen balloons. There are many creative possibilities using the stuffed animal balloon arrangements. We learned that the secret to selling them quickly is that they must always be attractively *wrapped* in cellophane with a bow on top. The key elements to doing one effectively are to: a) use very plush and *soft* stuffed animals, b) cut a cardboard platform and wrap it with silver or gold foil (obtainable at most party supply stores), c)wrap platform and stuffed animal with clear cellophane from the bottom up and d) tie the ends of the cellophane together with a big attractive bow. Top the entire arrangement by attaching a half dozen rainbow bouquet of balloons of red, orange, yellow, green, blue, and purple or pastels of hot rose, peach, yellow, wintergreen, pale blue, and lilac. If you buy your stuffed animals of high quality and at good prices, your total cost for an arrangement such as this can be as little as $15. You can easily sell them from $40 to $50. Two very good suppliers of very fine stuffed animals are Russ Berrie and Company, Inc. and Windor Toys, Inc. You may call or write them respectively for their color catalogs by contacting:

Russ Berrie and Company, Inc.
Corporate Headquarters: Oakland, New Jersey
1+800+631-8465
(In New Jersey 1+800+222-1160

OR

Windor Toys, Inc
140 Grand Street
Carlstadt, New Jersey 07072
(201) 935-8989

The basic idea behind pricing your merchandise correctly is to charge *at least* twice what it costs your to produce the gift. If the gift costs you $20 to produce, charge at least $40, however $50 is even better if you think your market is willing to pay the price. See illustration for examples of some of these exciting stuffed animal balloon arrangement concepts:

Stuffed Animal Balloon Arrangements

34

The other major type of the balloon arrangement in use falls under the category of:

Table Centerpieces

This is book about becoming a balloon artist. Becoming a balloon artist also involves knowing how to artistically and tastefully decorate the *tables* of large celebrations such as wedding receptions, banquets, anniversaries, bar-mitzvahs, and other major functions. Until the advent of balloon artistry on a very serious level, flowers pretty much dominated the decorating scene. In planning for a wedding, for example, you would traditionally plan for the wedding gown, photographer, caterer, cake, and flowers. Now you're hearing people plan for the wedding gown, photographer, caterer, cake, flowers, and *balloons*. I have consistently observed over the course of my many years in this business that people are ordering balloons *along with* flowers more. This is not to say that I feel that it is the destiny of balloons to take the *place* of flowers because I feel that there is a need and room for *both* industries. But it is an undeniable fact that the force and influence of the balloon is seen and felt on every front. Florists to a great degree now are beginning to see the potential of balloons as they begin to incorporate more and more balloons along with their flower designs. In the seminars that I give around the country on balloon decorating, florists make up at least 50% of my students. If you know anything about flowers, flowers *and* balloons are the best way to go.

Table centerpieces for major banquet events may be done with balloons and flowers or done exclusively with balloon centerpiece concepts. One of the basic principles of successful decorating is to use a "center of focus" or main design concept such as the weave/King-7 combination (explained in later chapters). After doing the main design concept, balloons are then placed on each guest table. The recommended number of balloons per table is usually 3. (Sometimes it's 4). But 3 balloons per table is pretty much standard. If your client is having a small floral arrangement on each table, then you simply attach 3 color-coordinated 11" balloons with matching ribbon onto the floral arrangements and charge $3 per table (roughly $1.00 per balloon). However, *never* tell a client you are charging by balloon but *by design*. This is a *must* in successfully quoting prices. If the person has 30 tables and plans to have floral arrangements, you say something like, "Your tables will be $90 to do."

When I say color coordinated, you color coordinate with the colors of the bridal party. If the bridal party plans to use pink and white then you attach 2 pink balloons and 1 white or 2 white balloons and 1 pink onto the floral arrangement. Ask your client which of the above combinations they would prefer best. No matter which combination they choose, they have chosen *balloons*.

There will be also those clients who want to do it all in balloons, not using flowers at all. We have countless clients such as these. To do a table centerpiece, be sure to have something elegant and attractive with just enough weight to hold the balloons down. Three of the most successful designs offered by Balloons by Prosper is: 1)the *Candle - Bow Centerpiece Arrangement* which is comprised of a simple floral glass vase into which is placed a cellophane wrapped candle (to prevent anyone from lighting it) and finished off with an attractive color-coordinated bow at the neck of the vase onto which are attached 3 color-cordinated balloons 2) the *Ceramic Swan Arrangement* which is comprised of a white ceramic swan placed on a silver or gold foil-wrapped cardboard platform adorned at its edges with Hershey's kisses as well as the kisses placed in the hollow back of the swan all wrapped in clear cellophane with a big matching bow on the top onto which are attached 3 balloons, and 3) the *Chamay Sparkling Non-Alcoholic Grape Cider Arrangement* in the silver or gold label which is comprised of an elegant champagne-looking bottle which is mounted on foil-wrapped cardboard, lined with a kind of gold coin caramels and wrapped in cellophane and topped with a bow onto which also are attached 3 color-coordinated balloons. We sell these 3 centerpiece arrangements respectively for $8, $15, and, $18. Multiply $15 times 30 tables and you'll come up with $450-*just for the tables only*!

Table Centerpiece Designs

You can find floral glass vases, bows, and candles at most party supply centers. Ideas and items such as the white ceramic swan may also be found at your better party supply centers. The Chamay sparkling imported grape juice can be obtained by calling or writing:

Boyd Wilson International
Castro Valley, California 94546
(415) 881-0448

The idea of using non-alcoholic items such as these very elegant looking bottles of Chamay sparkling grape juice is that you side-step the problems of having to obtain a liquor license and you also are able to offer these centerpiece designs for adolescent events such as sweet 16's and the Jewish bar-mitzvah's which celebrate the making of 13 years old. Non-alcohlic champagne-looking items work out excellently for gift deliveries also. A bottle of Chamay imported sparkling French grape juice will cost you about $3.00.

These are just some of our many new ideas that are taking the party planning scene by storm.

Chapter Five
THE KING-7

We have a particular design formula that goes on the main table seen at weddings, banquets, and anniversaries. A main table area usually is comprised of two nine-foot tables put together an covered with a fancy tablecloth. Over this setting, we put a weave arch (explained in Chapter 7) and a set of 3 *King*-7 balloons in the middle. What is a King-7? A King-7 is probably one of the most exciting design concepts we have discovered. A King-7 is a diamond clear 16" balloon, with seven 5" balloons placed in the inside, grouped in a set of 3, and attached to an attractive base like a white ceramic swan or some type of glass or crystal base to weigh the bouquet down. We call it a King-7 because it is a *king*-size balloon (16") with 7 smaller balloons (5") in the inside. Thus, we have a *King*-7 balloon. When Estela first discovered the mechanics of getting the smaller balloons inside the large 16" clear, she had some doubts as to how well this new technique would be received by the public. The King-7 was an *instant* success. People just loved it. You would always hear the question in tones of great fascination as soon as the guests would arrive, "How in the world do they get those little balloons inside that big one!" This bouquet design has the same enchantment of a ship-in-the-bottle. We learned quickly that the King-7 was the ideal design as an accompaniment to the weave on the main table. So successful is this combination that we *always* offer the weave/King-7 as a *set*. One goes with the other.

The King-7

40

The King-7 bouquet is always done in a group of 3 and placed on the *main* table to create the greatest impact.

The question of course which is going through your mind right now is "How on earth *do* you get seven inflated 5-inch balloons inside of *one* 16-inch balloon?" It takes just a little dexterity and a few nights practice to become a King-7 expert. Here's how it's done.

Get a new pencil (without a point) and place the *flat* writing end (the end opposite the eraser) into an uninflated 5" balloon with your right hand. Momentarily hold the 5" balloon and pencil in position between the thumb and index finger. Now inflate the 16" diamond clear balloon to about 1/2 it's full-blown capacity with your left hand. Bracing the pencil against your chest or abdomen, push the 5" balloon into the partially inflated 16" clear. You might lose a little helium out of your 16" clear balloon in the pushing process, but don't let that bother you. Now with your left thumb and forefinger, pinch the two balloons together as you briskly pull the pencil out with your right hand, leaving a 5" uninflated balloon inserted 3/4's of the way inside the partially inflated 16" clear. You are now holding the tips of the two balloons together with your left hand. Here comes the tricky part. While holding these two balloons together in between the tips of your thumb and index finger of your left hand, with your *right* hand, pull out slightly the tips of the 5" balloon and inflate it to a *round* but not an over-inflated pear-shape. You must gently release the thumb and index finger of your left hand enough for helium to go into the 5" balloon while not losing too much helium out of the 16" balloon. You must get a *feel* for how much you need to press your finger tips together and when and how you should release. At this point, it is beyond explanation it is something you must *do*. It is a matter of learn by doing. You now pull the 5" tip out as far as it will comfortably stretch an tie a knot onto it with your right hand while still holding on to the 16" balloon with your left hand. Using the cutting blade of your valve, cut off the tip of the 5" balloon. Your first inflated 5" balloon should now be in the inside. Repeat exactly the same process for the other six balloons. After placing your seventh and final balloon in the inside, blow your 16" to its proper full capacity. Attach a nice ribbon (preferably a ribbon one inch wider than you typically use with an ordinary balloon arrangement). Now put on a fancy bow at the neck of the balloon. With 3 King-7 balloons finished, you tie them to a base arrangement like a floral vase of glass or white ceramic. It is always in taste and decorative style to place a big bow on your vase as well.

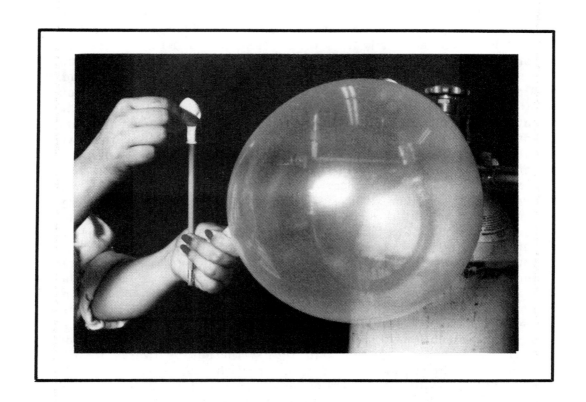

Doing A King-7
Step 1

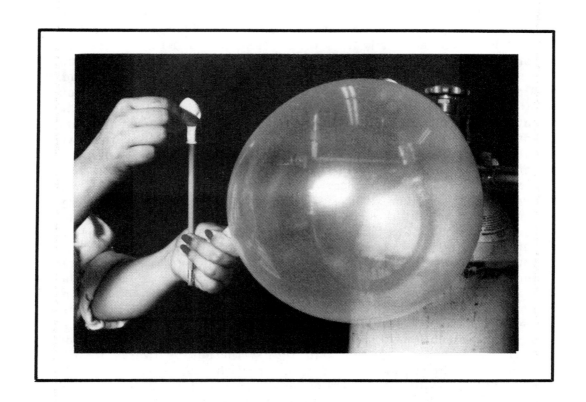

Doing A King-7
Step 1

Doing A King-7
Step 2

Doing A King-7
Step 3

44

Doing A King-7
Step 4

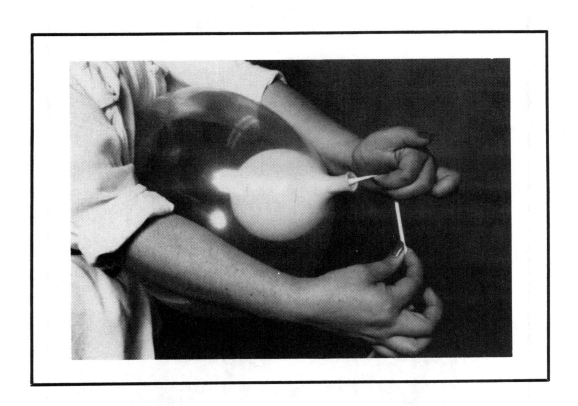

Doing A King-7
Step 5

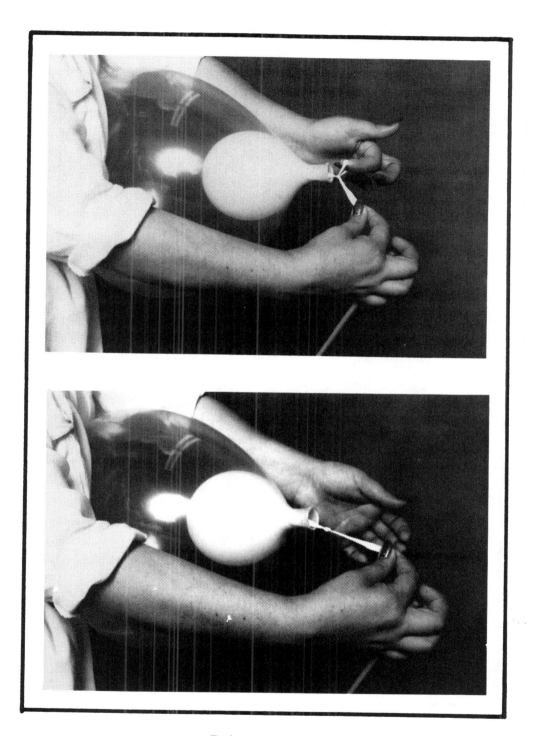

Doing A King-7
Step 6

47

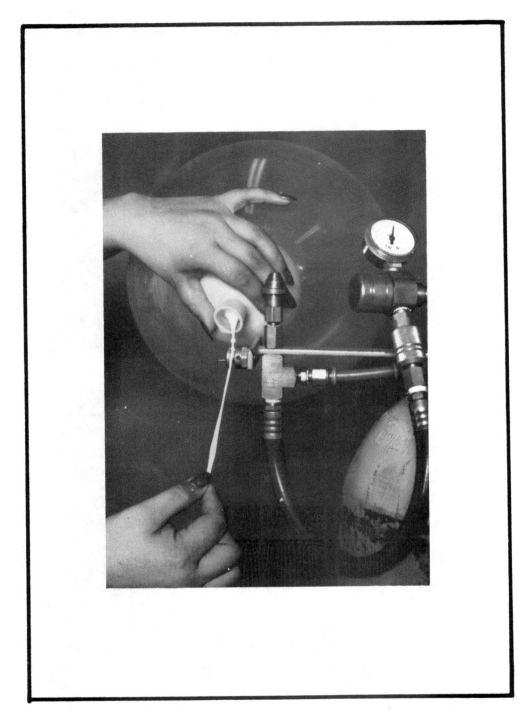

Doing A King-7
Step 7

48

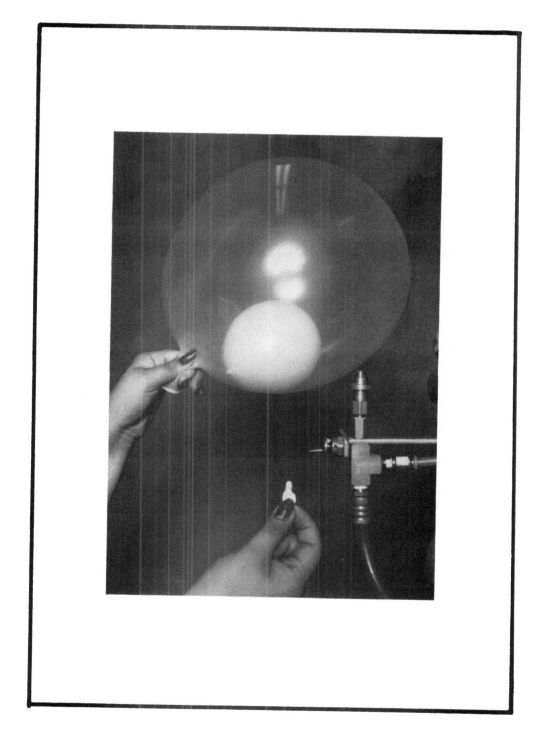

Doing A King-7
Step 8

Sometimes while attempting to inflate the 5" balloon, you notice that it begins to inflate in the tip or entrance of the 16" balloon rather than inside the balloon. This is because you have not pushed your 5" balloon up and inside far enough. Sometimes a 5" balloon will pop inside the 16" clear as you are inflating it. To remove the popped balloon simply stretch the tip of the 16" clear creating a type of funnel through which the pieces may fall to the bottom and you may then easily remove with your thumb and index finger. You are also probably wondering, since we are using helium, if the 5" balloons on the inside will float. No. If the 16-inch *"mother"* balloon pops then the seven 5-inch balloons on the inside, like liberated little cherubs, take to the skies and float gently up to the heavens. It has something to do with atmospheric pressure. The atmospheric pressure on the inside of the 5" balloons is the same as the clear balloon in which it inhabits. Once on the outside the heavier air *pushes* the lighter 5" balloons up.

You may also ask *why only 7 balloons*. Why not *10*? or 20. Or 50! Well, there's a very good reason. Through experience, we have learned that the optimum number is 7. In other words, adding more and more balloons will add more latex weight and will cause your King-7 to come down faster. Doing no more than seven balloons on the inside will allow a 20 to 24 hour floating life.

In Chapter 7, The Art of Color Combination, you will learn how to color coordinate the 5" balloons of your King-7.

One last thing before we wrap this chapter up is a bit of advice: *Try not to do a King-7 balloon in front of anyone.* Have your helpers do them on the outside or in some hidden room, *then* bring them in to the reception hall or decoration area all finished and done. Doing it this way you will preserve all of the magic and mystique of those who will see it for the first time.

"How in the world do they get those little balloons inside that big one!" Smile.

Chapter Six
THE SINGLE ARCH

It is surprising to most people when I tell them that the most lucrative, the most simple, and the most misunderstood and/or poorly done technique is *the single arch.* The single arch is basically a string of 11" helium filled balloons that are clipped onto a curling ribbon one after the other in as many as 40 or 50 balloons per row. They are equally spaced using a plastic disc and the disc-tyer needle of your valve. The balloons lightly touch each other - not too tightly pressed and not too separate. Where most so-called decorators fall flat on their faces doing the single arch is in allowing too much space in-between the balloons leaving them looking like gapped teeth smiling upward toward the ceiling. A single arch should be done with the same care and artistic sensitivity as would be done in any advanced or intricate weave-design. Artistic care and detail is something that shows through in even the simplest of balloon arrangements.

The single arch gets its power and beauty from being used correctly in combination *with other* single arches. I have seen individuals many times try to decorate with using, for example, *one* single arch over a main table or maybe one arch over an entrance area. It's nice, but it just doesn't create any visual *whallop!* No *ooh's* and *aah's* are evoked which is the purpose of all balloon artistry.

Design Formulas

We now come to a concept that I teach in all of my balloon decorating seminars-*the design formula.* Briefly stated, a design formula is a design concept which is easily reproduced, artistically sound, and proven to be a consistent seller. The most classic design formula of the single arch concept is the 6-Arch Tunnel Design. The 6-Arch Tunnel is *always* done over the dance area. I do this design repeatedly for weddings, bar-mitzvahs, and anniversaries. After having done so many of these and in so many different situation, I have come to the conclusion that you never really have to do more than 45 or 50 balloons per arch. Forty balloons per arch is about average for almost all dance floors.

The secret to quoting prices is to always quote price *by design*. You show a client a photo of a 6-Arch Tunnel, for example, and you say "This design is $250 (plus tax)." For your purposes of pricing, *you* know that what you are charging comes out to be about $1.00 per balloon, but you would never tell a *client* that. If you say that you are charging by balloon instead of by design, you have reduced your art to the level of the cost per balloon. The client sees you now not as a balloon *designer* working with *ideas and imagination* but rather a balloon *vendor* working with balloon disc, and string. There is nothing wrong with being looked upon as a balloon vendor. That's how I started out. But if you are looked upon as a balloon artist, a balloon designer, or a balloon decorator, you will almost *automatically* be able to command more money.

The 6-Arch Tunnel

Doing A Single Arch

This technique can be done with one person, but for a smoother flow of movement, I recommend that you work with at least one other person. To do your single arch, you will need: a bag of plastic discs, a disc tyer (found on your valve), curling ribbon, foil covered bricks, and 11" balloons.

Place your spool of ribbon on the floor and pull a line of ribbon up to your valve. Inflate your 11" balloon. Leave about 2 feet of slack from the start of your ribbon; your first balloon will begin here. Have your helper place one plastic disc onto the disc tyer. (Your helper will also now begin to inflate and hand over to you all of your balloons.)

You now align about 2 inches of the ribbon across the top of an outstretched balloon tip. Place the balloon and string on top of the end tip of your disc tyer needle and pull downward with your left hand and with the index and middle finger of your right hand, pull the clip over and down onto the ribbon and balloon tip as far as it will go.

Clipping The Single Arch
Step 1

55

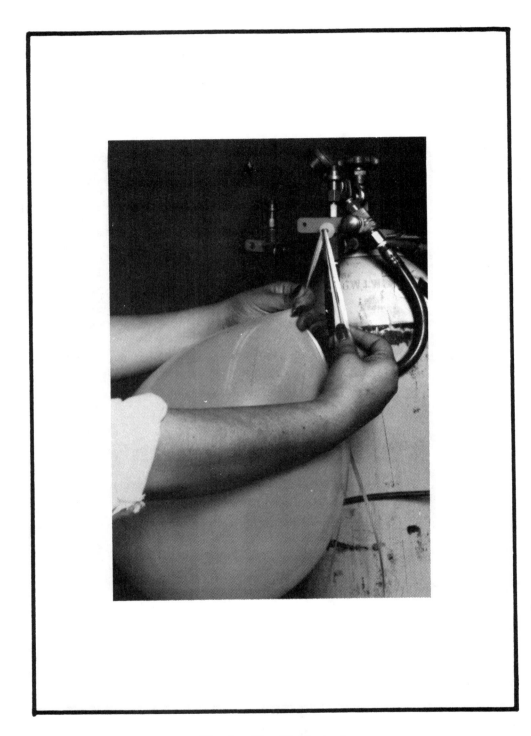

Clipping The Single Arch
Step 2

Clipping The Single Arch
Step 3

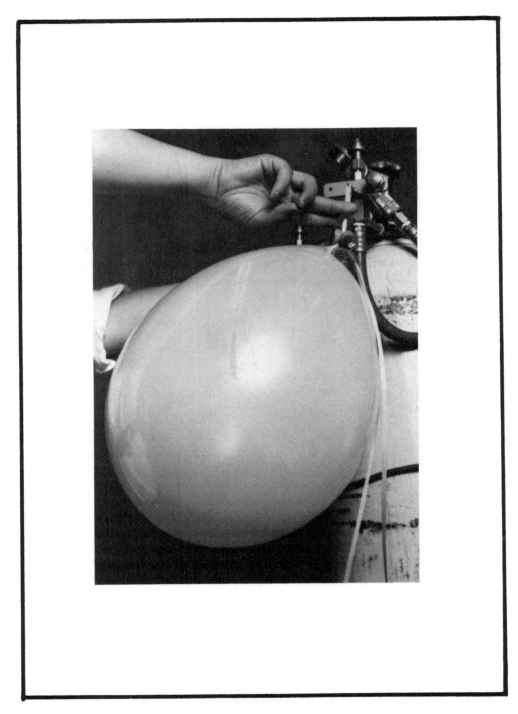

Clipping The Single Arch
Step 4

Clipping The Single Arch
Step 5

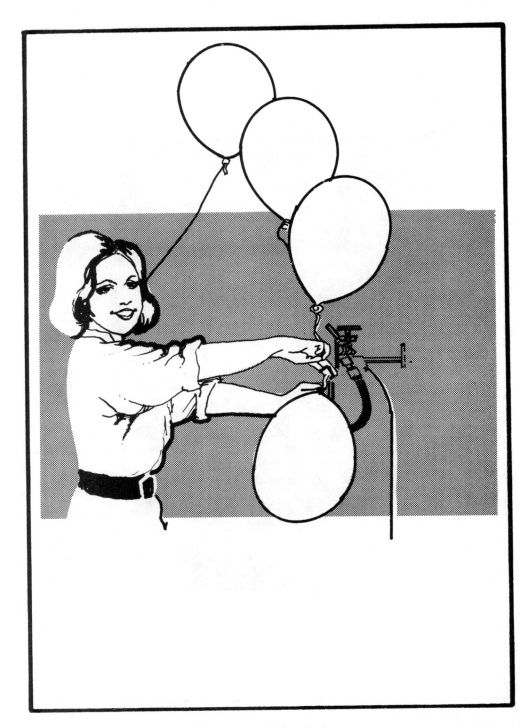

Clipping The Single Arch
Step 6

Once your first balloon is clipped, attach the next balloon about a foot apart. This is not to say that you are to whip out your tape measure to mark off 12 inches. This measuring process is all done by sight and your skill as an artist comes by not placing them too close together or too far apart.

Each time you clip on a balloon, your balloon line floats higher and higher into the air. Somewhere around the 10th balloon, you should tie the top of the balloon line onto the leg of a banquet chair. Now the line suddenly curves and you see the beginning of your balloon arch. You continue clipping on the balloons in the same fashion attempting to space each balloon, one from the other, so that they are not pressing nor gapped wide apart but rather *lightly touching each other*. This is where most would-be decorators fail. Their single arches are either wide chasms or pressed so close until they are crooked. As you continue to attach more and more balloons onto your ribbon, the arch will start moving up high toward the ceiling. When this starts to happen, you simply have your helper move the chair back and away from you. In this way, you can watch the complete formation of your single from beginning to end.

Let us assume that you are doing a 45-balloon arch that is one of a total of 6 arches that you will build over a dance area. Upon completion of your 45 balloons, have your helper wrap in silver aluminum foil 2 plain concrete bricks that you can get from any major hardware store for about 20 cents each. These 2 foil wrapped bricks will serve as the end weights or bases of your single arches. Now cut off the ribbon end from the chair and tie it securely around one of the two bricks. Cut off the other end of the arch attached to the umbilical cord-like spool of curled ribbon. With this free end, you tie it to the other brick base. Your single arch is just about finished. I say just about finished because there is one final step to completion.

Grooming-Adjusting Your Balloons

Grooming is the process of closing up wide gaps between some balloons and giving a little more space to other overtightened balloons until your entire row of balloons are all *lightly* touching. The secret to closing or widening the balloons of your single arch *after* they are all placed together, lies in grabbing *lightly*, the little loop of ribbon that you will notice on the underside of the arch lying directly under each balloon at the point where the balloon-tip and ribbon are attached into the round plastic disc. By placing your index finger

61

into this loop and pulling on it from side to side, you will notice that the two above balloons will begin to close more and more as you continue to pull on the loop. After all balloons are groomed and lightly touching, check to see that some of the loops are not hanging down like large appendages. If you happen to have an enlarged and distracting loop hanging from under some of your balloons, tie the loop in a small and simple knot so that it disappears again under each balloon. Once you have finished each arch with the grooming process, you may now pat yourself on the back and look yourself *straight in the eye* before any mirror and call yourself a true balloon artist.

Don't Tape Arches To Floor

In our early days of decorating, we used to tape the single arches to the floor using an industrial strength clear plastic tape. The tape worked just fine to hold the single arches to the floor until it was time for the custodian to remove it later. On wood finished floors, the tape worked so well until it ripped off the varnish also. After getting a few nasty calls from irate hall owners, we soon desisted in this practice coming up with the much faster and more practical method of using bricks.

If you are doing a 6 arch tunnel design over the dance area, place one of the creative centerpiece designs as explained in Chapter 4 on each of the guest-tables. The perfect accompaniment for the center of the *main* table would be a set of 3 King-7 balloons attached to an attractive floral glass vase and bow.

Next chapter, we are going to cover one of the most essential and intrinsically breathtaking technique of balloon artistry - *the weave technique*.

Chapter Seven

THE WEAVE

The magic of the spiral weave was first woven by Treb Heining (the father of professional balloon decorating) back in 1976 and since then many enthusiasts and admirers of balloon art have been trying to unlock the secrets of its creation. Some have succeeded to a great degree, but for many others, the *how* of its beauty still *remains* a secret.

In 1980, not having any books on the subject nor seminars on the how-to of balloon technique, I set out to re-discover this secret for myself. I bought a set of kid's Playdough in several different colors. I rolled-up in my hands about 40 little pink balls of Playdough making sure they were all the same size. I then pressed four of these small balls together until they formed a sort of four-leaf-clover-look (without the stem). This was my first section. Immediately on top of that, I placed another 4-balled section made the same way as the first. Then on top of this, I placed another, then another on top of this another and so on until I had a stack of 10 sections of carefully rolled clay balls. This little clay sculpture was the exact replica of a balloon weave *without the spiral*. I then took a marker and traced a line where I thought a spiral *should* be along the clay bumps from top around to bottom. Seeing where a spiral should be, I then surgically removed *only* the balloons which were marked on the spiral line. Here I inserted clay balls of a *yellow* color and there, before me, was a spiral clay column. The final step to discover how this spiral was geometrically forming itself from the first level to the next was to look a-top at the first section keeping my eye at the position of each *succeeding* yellow ball. I removed the top section and noticed that the yellow ball of the second section had moved its position one ball to the right. Removing the second section, the yellow ball was in a position one ball further, moving in a circular pattern. Removing the third second, I saw the yellow ball positioned in the fourth section one more to the right continually moving in the same direction. Upon taking off the fourth section, I saw the yellow ball in the original first section position. I had discovered the secret of the spiral and went on to utilize and perfect this same principal in *balloon* weaving.

Doing The Perfect Weave

To do the perfect weave you must first start with proper equipment followed by perfect technique. Let us take a look at your basic balloon weave equipment. These are: 9" balloons, paper clips (standard size), natural twine, and 2 foiled-wrapped concrete bricks.

Unroll your twine, and look around the room to find any sufficiently weighted object onto which you may tie this end. You may use the leg of a 9 foot banquet table, the iron railing of a low balcony area, or the metal rod handle that is used to push open exit doors in hotels and churches. You keep unrolling the twine out to about 40 feet making sure that it is tightly outstretched. Cut it at this point with a pair of scissors and tie this end securely onto the handle bar of your helium tank hand-truck. The purpose of tying it onto your hand truck is to be able to continually *move* the twine outward as the helium starts to make the weave rise up at the middle.

The Helix

The next step to forming your weave is to do the first section or as it is called in professional balloon decorating: your first *helix*. A helix is formed by attaching 5 or 6 nine inch balloons onto a standard size paper clip. Remember, you use *9" balloons only* to do your weaves, and the secret to perfect symmetry and balance is to watch out for overinflation. Blow all balloons up exactly the same size. I have seen some monstrous weaves done with 11" balloons that were grotesquely overinflated.

Inflating your first 9" balloon, you hand-tie a quick and easy knot and place it in between the side of your right knee and your helium cylinder which is chained to your hand truck that outstretches the twine. Lean lightly on the knotted balloon with your knee allowing it not to escape and float up to the ceiling. Make sure that the balloon tip *faces* the person who does the clipping so that he or she can grab it easily. Though a *6 balloon* helix is done in certain techniques such as in doing the Balloon People seen in Chapter 12 or in doing a 6 color swirl for a complete rainbow spiral weave, the *standard* and proper number for doing most weaves that you will do for inside or outside decorating is a *5-balloon helix*.

Blow up your second balloon in the same manner as you did the first, making sure that it is slightly under-inflated, that is, round in shape and exactly the same size as the first. The third, fourth, and fifth balloons are all done the same. You one-by-one align all of the balloons between the outside of your right leg and the helium cylinder starting from your knee up to your hip.

Tying and Holding Balloons

Clipping The Balloons On

The person doing the clipping, slightly opens the paper clip and inserts the opened end portion into the inner tip of each of the five balloons pushing them down into the bottom portion or "well" of the paper clip. See illustration, page 68.

Holding The Helix

Having placed all 5 balloons onto the paper clip, you must make sure all 5 balloon tips are held and pushed down into the bottom or inner well portion of the paper clip by holding your helix clip with the thumb and index portion of your right (or left) hand.

Starting at the end three feet from your helium tank, you attach your first helix. In practice, two or three people can and should work a weave: One person blows and ties each balloon, a second person clips the balloons together and places them onto the twine, and a third person *weaves* and tightens each helix one after the other. Remember a helix is a *section* of 5 balloons clipped together. Attach the helixes onto the twine by placing the outstretched twine in between the slightly opened clip all of the way onto the bottom inner portion of the paper clip then closing up the outer opened portion. See illustration, page 69.

Attaching The Helix

Don't forget that you must always hold the top portion of your paper clip keeping all 5 balloons into the bottom inner well of the clip with your thumb and index finger.

With your first helix in place, you now begin to *weave* the balloons around the twine so that they are *snug* enough to stay in place but loose enough to slide back and forth along the twine, that is, you want to tighten them but not tighten them too much. Moving them around the twine a few times, you tighten maybe 2 or 3 balloons. Move your helix a little (holding it by the clip); if it moves easily but snugly, it's probably tight enough. If you can barely move it, it's *too* tight. (Since your first and last helix form the structure or *sandwich* of all of the other helixes, these two helixes only should be tightened *very securely* so as they don't move). See illustration, page 70.

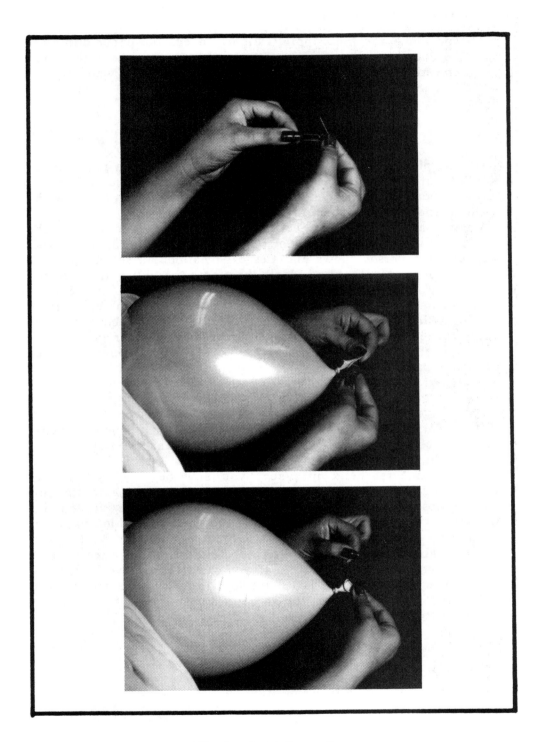

Clipping the Balloons On

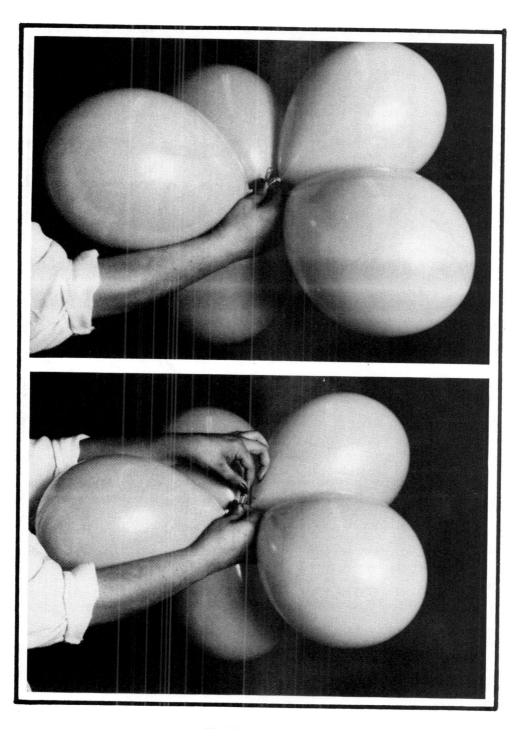

Holding the Helix

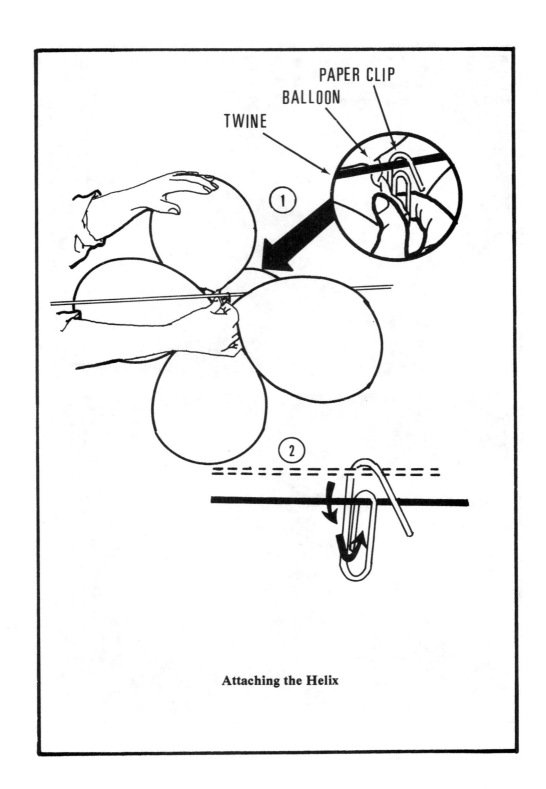

PAPER CLIP

BALLOON

TWINE

① ②

Attaching the Helix

Weaving The Helix

After your first helix is woven snugly in place, grab hold of your second helix and tighten it onto the twine as you did the first. Do the same with the third, fourth and fifth helix. Having five helixes tightened up, you now must push them into place by flattening out helix number one with your left hand and pushing helix number two into position with your right hand. See illustration, page 72.

Pushing Helixes In Place

If you notice your first flattened out helix, you will see the spaces or "V" grooves where two balloons touch each other. It is into these spaces or *grooves* where the balloons of the *following* helix will be pushed in place awaiting the next helix. Each helix with the exception of the first·and last rests in the grooves of a preceding helix and at the same time serves as a brace for the following one. See illustration, page 73.

Positioning Helixes

When you push a helix in the corresponding spaces of the preceding one, be sure that they are pushed snugly together without allowing a lot of space in between them.

Now we will get into the mechanics of doing a *spiral* weave. See illustration, page 74.

Doing A Spiral Weave

A spiral weave follows all of the principles of the solid color weave with the exception of something that we call *"following a helix color formula."* A helix color formula is the number and pattern of colors which must be followed as each helix is put in place. More balloons per helix will allow more colors per helix, that is a 5 balloon helix will allow you up to five different colors if so desired, and a 6 balloon helix will allow you up to 6 different colors. A 5-balloon helix is the *standard*. Let us look at a helix color formula that will create a spiral.

71

Weaving the Helix

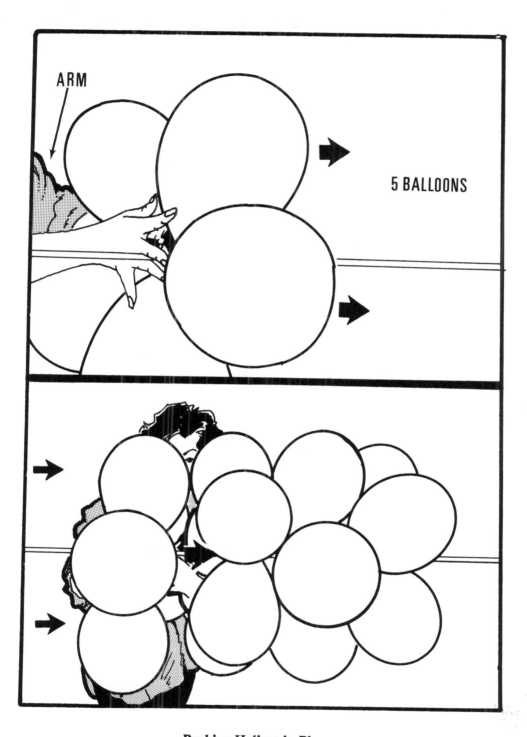

Pushing Helixes in Place

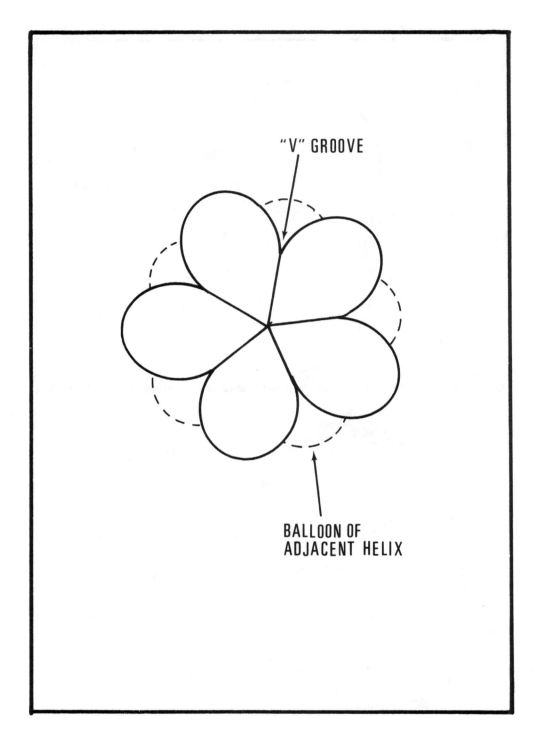

"V" GROOVE

BALLOON OF
ADJACENT HELIX

Positioning Helixes

Helix Color Formula:
(2 pinks, 2 whites, and 1 red)

Let us assume that we are decorating for a Valentine's Day wedding. The client says that she wants to use the colors red, pink, and white. A very elegant helix color formula could be 2 pinks, 2 whites, and 1 red. The 2 pink balloons are side-by-side. The 2 white balloons follow next to each other, and then we have the red balloon.

The secret behind doing the spiral is to be sure you maintain the color *order* of your chosen helix color formula and visually follow the clockwise movement (to the right) of any *one* balloon. For this example, you might follow the circular clockwise movement of the clear balloon. The idea is to notice where the clear balloon is positioned in the first helix. As you slide the second helix into place, positioned the clear balloon of the second helix to the *immediate right* of the clear balloon of the first helix. The clear balloon of the third helix is placed to the *immediate right* of the clear balloon of the second helix. The clear balloon of the fourth helix is placed to the *immediate right* of the clear balloon of the third helix and the clear balloon of the fifth helix is placed to the *immediate right* of the clear balloon of the fourth helix. With the fifth helix your colors will have made its first of several complete spirals around your weave. You continue placing all of your helixes in this same manner until you have completed your desired weave length. If you were doing a weave of 50 helixes with 5 balloons per helix, you would have a total of 10 continuous color swirls or spirals. See illustration, page 76.

Twisting The Colors

To quickly and easily create the spiral pattern as you are placing one helix on top of another is to always follow the movement of any one balloon of your helix color formula. In the above example, we follow the movement of the *red* balloon one successive position to the right with each additional helix placement. We could have just as easily followed the movement of one of the 2 pinks or one of the 2 whites. See illustration, page 77.

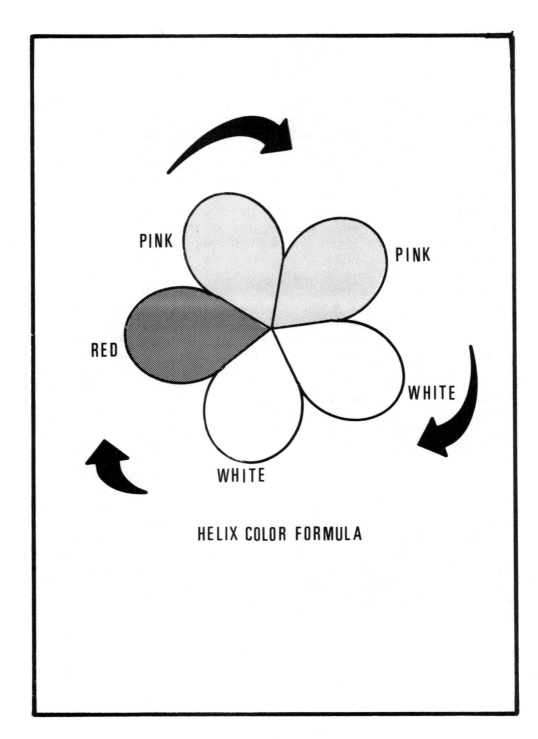

Helix Color Formula
(2 pinks, 2 whites, and 1 red)

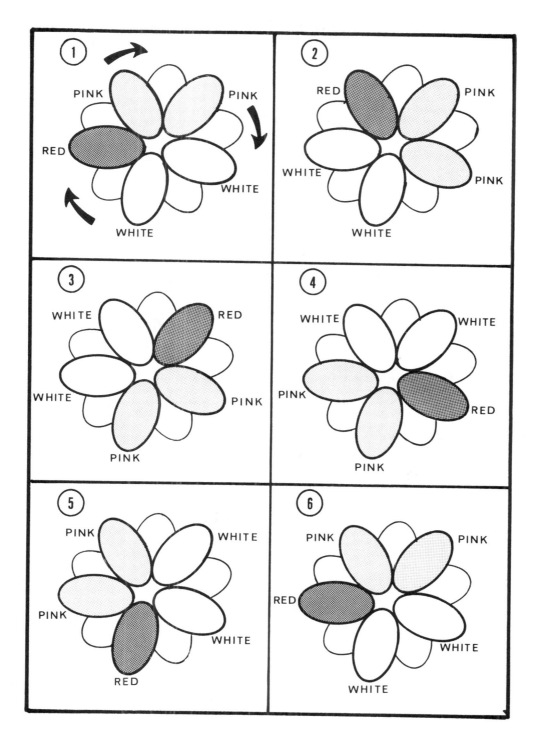

Twisting the Colors

The number of helix color formulas possible are many and creative combinations are at your disposal. Following are examples of a few others that I have successfully used:

HELIX COLOR FORMULA

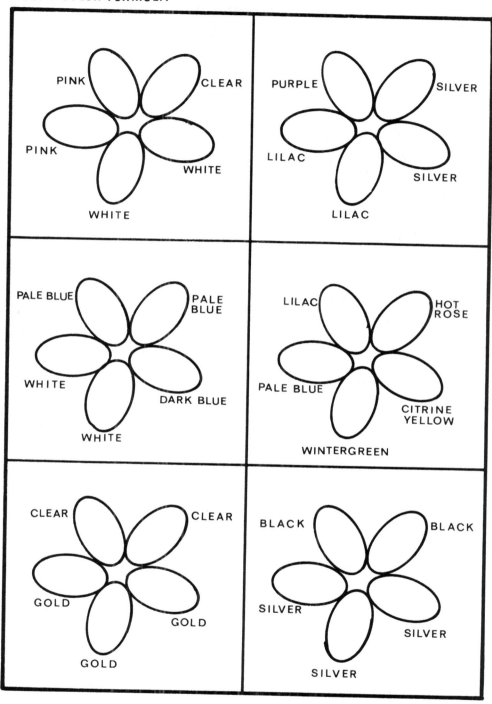

Helix Color Formulas

The Sectional Weave

Aside from solid color weaves and spiral weaves there is still one more weave pattern technique. This is called the sectional weave. A sectional weave uses different *solid color helixes* placed in a pre-designed and orderly fashion. An example of a good sectional weave is the clear-color-clear pattern. For example, you first place a helix of all clear balloons, then you follow by placing a solid color helix (let's say a helix of all gold). Follow with a helix of all clear, then a helix of all gold, then all clear. Continue in this pattern until you complete the number of desired helixes. Instead of gold, we could have easily substituted any bold or pastel color, and this color pattern formula would have worked just as effectively.

There is a very special sectional weave color formula which is called the Rainbow Sectional Weave which we will explain in depth in the next chapter - The Art of Color Combination.

Tying The Ends Of The Weave

After you have completed the specified number of helixes for your weave, the final step to completion is to tie up the ends of your weave and tie the remaining twine onto the foil-wrapped concrete bricks. To tie your weave ends, grab the twine of one end securely with your left hand and cut it with your right hand using a pair of scissors. Be sure that you have at least 5 feet of loose twine to work with. Slide your left hand along the twine into the center portion of the last helix in front of you. While holding on with your left hand, use your *right* hand to wrap the twine around the inside center of two or three balloons of this last helix in front of you. The purpose of doing this is to be sure that the end helixes which "sandwich" all of the inner helixes, do not slip out of place. With still sufficient slack on this piece of twine, you tie it securely and closely as possible to your first foil-wrapped brick. You may now place the first complete end on the floor held securely by your brick base.

End Tying

When you complete one end, go through exactly the same procedure for the other end.

With both brick bases attached and on the floor, you now get your helper to lift one end of the weave while you lift the other and you both place it on top of a main table. With a set of 3 King-7 balloons in the middle, you have a *winning* design arrangement. See illustration, page 84.

Formula For Pricing Weave

To effectively and profitably sell a weave, you must know how to correctly price it. Since the majority of your designs will involve a main table, and since the majority of main table areas are comprised of 2 nine-foot standard banquet tables side-by-side and draped with a table cloth, you can always do the *standard* main table weave size of 42 helixes. A standard main table weave of 42 helixes is $155. Since I always offer a weave *and* three King-7 balloons as a *set* for the main table, I will simply explain to my client that to do a weave over a main table is $180 (plus tax) and the King-7 set goes with it.

There are indeed weave designs that you may want to do that will involve much more than a standard 42 helixes for a main table. The Chamber of Commerce might ask you to do a weave crossing over from one side of the street to the other as a finishing line marker for an outdoor marathon. *Now*, how do you quote a price? Easy. Here is a formula that you can use.

(LENGTH) X (HEIGHT FACTOR) X (CHARGE PER FOOT) = COST OF WEAVE

The *Length* is the length of the area measuring across in a straight line that the weave must cover, for example, one side of the street to the other. The *Height Factor* is a number constant of 2 which will always be 2 in this part of the formula because the weave really doesn't go across from one side to the other in a straight line but rather as a *curve* approximately twice the measurement of the length. The *Charge Per Foot* is the final part of the formula which is simply what *you* want to charge per estimated weave footage. Might I suggest between $4 and $5 per foot. I charge for most weaves about $4.25 per foot

Let us see how we would quote the price on a weave going from one side of the street to the other in the above example. Using a carpenter's retractable tape measure, we find that the width of the street is 50 feet. We know that the height factor is 2, and we are charging $4.25 per foot. So:

(LENGTH) X (HEIGHT FACTOR) X (CHARGE PER FOOT) = COST OF WEAVE

50 ft. X 2 X $4.25 = $425.00 (PLUS TAX)

The 4 Minute Mile And The 20 Minute Weave

Many of my seminar students will ask me, "Mr. Prosper, how long does it take to do a standard 42 helix weave over a main table?" For most beginners working with 2 helpers, I would say about 1 hour and a half to do it *right*. With practice you should be able to cut this time down to 45 minutes and eventually 1/2 hour. At the time of this writing, Estela, using 2 helpers, holds the 42-helix-weave record at 20 minutes. *You can never practice weave technique too much.* Like playing the piano, you only get better with practice.

Getting Balloons Off The Ceiling

In the course of doing a weave, one or two balloons are bound to slip loose and float up to the ceiling. *Clean all loose balloons off the ceiling.* Is this a job for *Superman*? Not quite. If you can't go up to the balloons, bring the balloons down to you. Inflate a 16" clear balloon. Get a spool of ribbon and tie it onto the balloon. Place two-way double stick tape in a crisscross pattern on top of the clear balloon. Raise the balloon up carefully while unrolling the spool of ribbon until you reach the area where the loose ceiling balloons are floating. Allow the taped tip of your 16" clear to touch and stick to the balloon that you want to retrieve and gently pull it down. Retrieve all other balloons in the same way then dispose of them. Using a 16" *clear* balloon you can see through to exactly where the tape is and 16 inches gives you more area to tape than a 9" or 11" balloon.

Once all balloons are cleaned off the ceiling, you are ready for your next decoration.

The Weave and King-7 Design

Chapter Eight
THE ART OF COLOR COMBINATION

It is very interesting that the very few individuals who do know how to do a fairly decent weave or single arch go somewhat astray when it comes to doing color coordination that is always satisfying to the sight.

The very first decoration I experimentally did was the classic 6 Single Arch Rainbow Tunnel. I didn't know it at the time, but this *first* decoration was actually a study in the basics of color coordination. The 6 single arch rainbow tunnel comprises itself of the six principal rainbow colors with each single row or arch being a different solid color in a specified and *unchangeable* order. The first row is all ruby red, the second row all orange, the third row all citrine yellow, the fourth row all standard green, the fifth row all sapphire blue, and the sixth and final row is all quartz purple. The next time you see a real rainbow, you will notice that it has the same color order. There is a quick and easy way to memorize the 6 colors and their proper order. Simple, remember the name ROY G. BIV. Who is this Roy G Biv character? Let's see:

> **R** - Red
> **O** - Orange
> **Y** - Yellow
>
> **G** - Green
>
> **B** - Blue
> *I* - *Indigo*
> **V** - Violet

For our purposes, we may ignore indigo, and violet is really purple.

There is also a very successful 6 arch *pastel* rainbow tunnel. Like the aforementioned *bold* rainbow colors, we have a pastel rainbow arch tunnel in the following sequence: one row of all *hot pink*, with the second row of *peach*, the third row *citrine yellow*, the fourth row *wintergreen*, the fifth row *pale blue*, and the sixth and final row *lilac*.

Rainbow Sectional Weaves

Rainbow combinations work quite well with weave technique also. A weave design for grand openings, ground breakings, and carnivals that I have sold many, many times is the Rainbow Sectional Weave.

The pastel weave can be used on the main table for a rainbow wedding. (Don't forget your pastel colored set of 3 King-7's in the middle.) The numbers alongside each color in the illustration indicate the number of solid colored helixes for each color and where their position should be. If you'd like to see just how beautiful this color design formula should be, get a set of crayons or a set of different colored felt markers and color in the illustration.

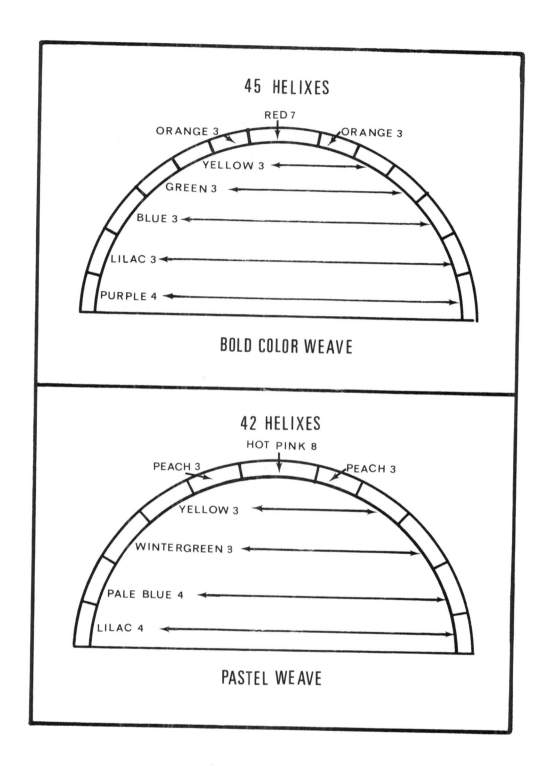

45 HELIXES

RED 7

ORANGE 3   ORANGE 3

YELLOW 3

GREEN 3

BLUE 3

LILAC 3

PURPLE 4

BOLD COLOR WEAVE

42 HELIXES

HOT PINK 8

PEACH 3   PEACH 3

YELLOW 3

WINTERGREEN 3

PALE BLUE 4

LILAC 4

PASTEL WEAVE

The Rainbow Sectional Weave

Color Combination For Weddings

The two most popular designs for weddings and elegant reception-like affairs is the 6 arch tunnel of single arches over the *dance* area and the weave/King-7 combination on the *main table*.

Whenever you are designing a wedding, the first thing that you must ask your client is "What are the wedding colors of your bridal party?" She will usually respond with naming some *pastel* color in combination with white. She will say: pink and white, lilac and white, light blue and white, peach and white, turquoise and white, or maybe even mint green and white. But you can be reasonably sure that she will mention some *pastel* and *white* which leads us to the basic color pattern formula of the 6 arch tunnel for weddings. This color formula is: (pastel-clear-white) + (pastel-clear-white). To illustrate this idea, let us take the combination of pink and white. The first row would be a row of all pastel (pink in this case), followed by a row of all clear, followed by a row of all white, followed again by the pink pastel, again a row of all clear, and finally a row of all white. Whatever the principal pastel color is, place it in the same position as the above example of pink and white.

When we speak of white there are actually *two types* of white that can be employed in the above formula. There is the *standard white* and the *metallic silver*. I include metallic silver as an elegant alternative because when blown up these balloons actually look like floating *pearls*. Hence, you would speak of two kinds of whites to your clients. You would offer them a choice of *pure white* or *pearl white*. Doesn't pearl white sound much more elegant than metallic silver?

If you are doing 6 single arches over the dance area and you have placed a balloon arrangement centerpiece on each of the guest-tables then a set of 3 King-7 balloons is a must for the center of the main table. (A weave *needs* a set of King-7, but a set of King-7 does not necessitate a weave). Combine the colors inside each of the King-7 balloons with the colors of the weave. In the case of a lilac and white weave, put 4 lilacs and 3 whites, 4 whites and 3 lilacs, or simply 7 lilacs inside each King-7. Remember you always place 7 five inch balloons inside of each 16" clear. (See Chapter 5 - The King-7 for the how-to of doing a King-7).

Color Metallics

While in the process of writing this book, Estela, my partner and chief design engineer, discovered a new and exciting way to create different colored metallic balloons. You combine an 11" metallic silver and an 11" balloon of any special tone color by inserting the special tone into the 11" metallic silver and inflate the *inside* 11" special tone. The special tone balloon will stretch the outside metallic silver and will create a special pearl-like hue of the inside color. These color metallic combinations are excellent for creating new varieties of balloon arrangements, wedding centerpieces - even weaves. Very interesting combinations are made when you insert any pastel color inside of the metallic silver.

The technique for doing this color metallic balloon is basically a one-step version of doing a balloon-inside-a balloon technique like the King-7 explained in Chapter 5. Simply take an 11" silver metallic and an 11" balloon of any particular color. Let's use wintergreen. In this case, you would take a pencil (just out of the box and with no point please) and insert the end opposite the eraser inside the 11" wintergreen all the way in. Now insert the 11" wintergreen all the way inside of the 11" metallic silver. While pressing the tips of both balloons with the thumb and index finger of your left hand, pull the pencil out quickly with your right hand. Inflate the inside wintergreen allowing it to stretch simultaneously the outside metallic silver. Holding the balloons with the first two fingers of your left hand, grab the tips of *both* balloons and tie a knot around both tips at the same time as you would a single balloon.

Doing the Color Metallic
Step 1

```
CONWIN CARBONIC COMPANY

Cust# MCCOLL  Reg#  1   User MIKE
Date 01/25/94 Time 10:38  Tckt#  47889
Item#              Qty   Price     Ext
------------------------------------------------

43840              1.00   4.00     4.00
FLOWERS& MAGAZINE
43828              1.00  37.00    37.00
MANUAL/ CHARLES PROSPER
52090              1.00  57.55    57.55
BRA2P
                                ----------
Subtotal                          98.55
Tax                                7.48
                                ==========
Total                            106.03

CASH                             111.05
Change received                    5.02

4510 SPERRY STREET, L.A.
```

Doing the Color Metallic
Step 2

Doing the Color Metallic
Step 3

We soon discovered something very interesting about the color metallic balloon. They actually last about 4 or 5 hours longer than a single 11" inflated balloon. By the fact that this is a *double* balloon, the helium inside has twice the trouble of finding a way to seep through the microscopic pores of the latex.

Before we move on to the next chapter, I thought you might like an interesting tidbit of information so that you won't be caught by surprise the next time you are doing a rainbow weave for some outside event. Did you know that honeybees and bumblebees flying high overhead will mistake your colorful rainbow weave below for an incredibly large and never before seen gigantic flower bursting to the seams with nectar. They will frantically zoom down in an enraptured state of anticipated delight only to find that this giant weave-like flower is deplete of any nectar and is dry, insipid, and rubbery. They'll whirl around in puzzled bewilderment and fly off angry, disillusioned, and confused. So, a word to the wise is sufficient. On the outside-BEE careful!

Chapter Nine

TECHNIQUES OF THE 5-INCH BALLOON

In the balloon decoration profession, I am amazed to find that virtually no one uses or knows how to use 5" balloon techniques to any great extent. One reason could be that most Qualatex distributors do not *carry* a wide variety of 5" balloons. I'm particularly talking about gross bags of the various standard and jewel tone colors in large quantities. If you're lucky, the majority of these distributors will carry only small quantities of the 5" standard assorted bags - which you do not want. The reason why so few Qualatex master distributors carry the 5" balloon is because so few balloonists request them or know how to use them. It's something like which came first the chicken or the egg. There is a way to get around this dilemma and that is to simply *request* that he start stocking them. If he responds that he can't because there is not a great demand for them, you can always have him special-order prepaid cases of the different colors of the 5" balloons that you will be using the most. A good bet would be to at least order a case of white, metallic silver, lilac, pink, pale blue, and clear. A case of 5" balloons usually contains about 24 gross, and the average cost per gross would be about $3.75. So you would be looking at about $90.00 per case plus shipping. Order only what you need at first, but eventually you will need all of the pastel and bold rainbow colors as well. Always order the jewel tones whenever possible.

The history of the use of the 5" balloon is a brief and modest one. It has been used mostly at carnivals as the balloon in front of the winning number at dart throw games. Creative uses of this unique balloon has almost totally been overlooked. The beauty of using the 5" balloon is that it is done always with *air* and all of it's designs will last for weeks and weeks at a time. Air inflated balloons of any size will always last longer than helium-filled balloons because air molecules are heavier and thicker than helium molecules and consequently will take longer to squeeze through the microscopic pores of the inflated latex surface. Five inch balloon techniques are also always hung from the top of something or against the surface of something and will necessitate the skillful use of 20 lb. monofilament plastic fish line, which you can find at almost any major sporting goods or hardware store. Next we see a *small* sample of the creative possibilities of the 5" balloon.

Five-Inch Balloon Designs

What's more, product cost for the 5" balloon techniques are low, and the profit margin is very high. Since you are basically using very inexpensive grosses of balloons and *air*, your only relatively initial expensive investment will be a Qualatex electric air inflator which will run you about $65.00 in most places. For example, to do a three-foot across wall heart as seen in the illustration, would take only 152 balloons, a little more than a $3.75 investment which is the cost of a 144 gross bag. This heart you can easily sell for about $95.00-a whopping profit margin!

To do a thorough treatise on 5" balloon weaving with it's numerous possibilities for doing letters, numbers, flags, hearts, and even company logos would require an entire book in itself. Each letter from A to Z and each number from 1 to 10 requires a specific set of instructions much beyond the scope of this chapter. However, I will go into the basics of mastering the 5" balloon weave which follow a close parallel to the 9" balloon weave techniques. To do a 5" balloon weave, you'll need a spool of 20 lb. monofilament fish-line, standard size paper clips, a Qualatex electric air inflator, and of course your 5" balloons. You will use only *4 balloons to a clip*, that is, a four-balloon helix. The secret, the real secret to doing gorgeous 5" balloon weaves is to blow up the balloons perfectly round and all the exact same size. Following exactly the same procedures of doing a 9" weave as explained in Chapter 7, you substitute *fish line* instead of twine. Knowing how many helixes are needed for a given design, you multiply this times 4 and you will know how many balloons you must inflate. Decide on your helix color formula, 3 lilac and 1 quartz purple for example and begin to blow up and tie your balloons. Get several large boxes so that you can blow up your balloon and quickly throw it into the box. Another person picks up the inflated balloons and places the appropriate four onto the paper clip then clips the helix onto the outstretched fish line. A third person begins to weave the helixes into place. Tie two or three balloons around the fish line a few times so that it is snugly in place but not too tight.

Working the 5" Weave
Step 1

Working the 5" Weave
Step 2

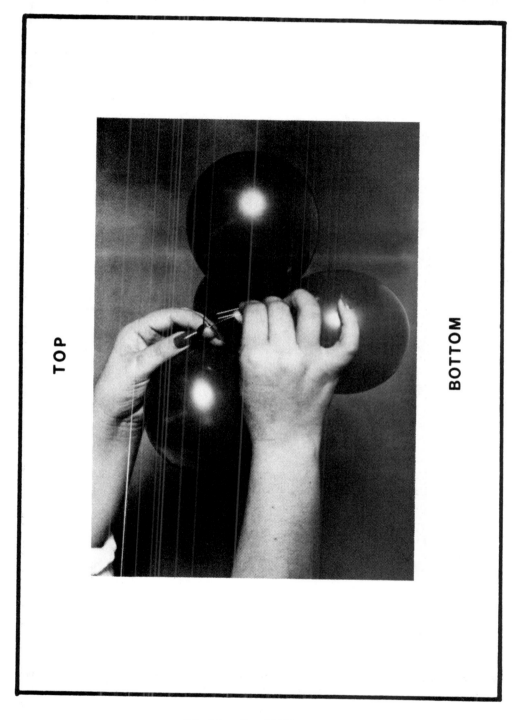

TOP

BOTTOM

Working the 5" Weave
Step 3

TOP

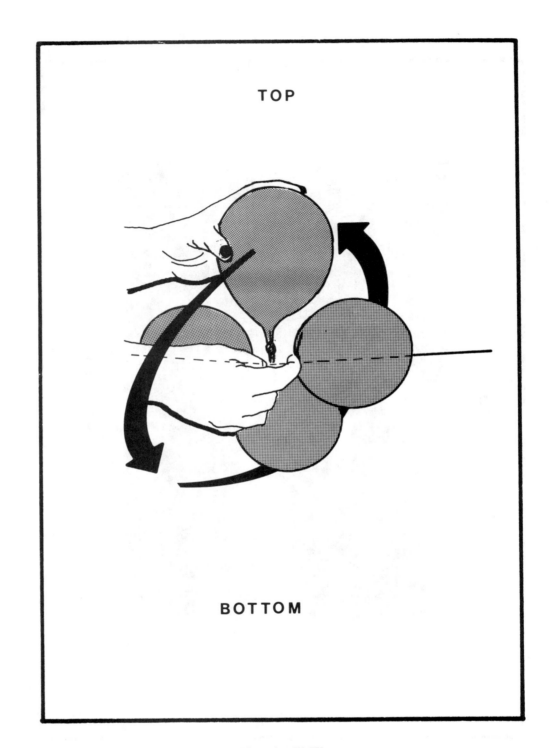

BOTTOM

**Working the 5" Weave
Step 4**

These designs are hung using 20 lb. fish line and a small tack. You basically wrap a piece of fish line around the top portion of your particular design, make a small loop at the fish line tip and nail a tack into the middle of the hoop right onto the wall where you want to hang it.

How To Price 5-Inch Balloon Designs

The time it takes you to do various designs employing the 5" weave technique will vary and you may even want to charge more according to the uniqueness of your design. As a general yardstick, however, $100 per every 30 helixes of design is a very fair asking price. Remember, 5" designs will last for weeks!

Using Lights Between Letters And Numbers

To create an even more stunning look you may also embed lights in between the helixes of your letters or numbers. The type of lights that you use are the standard lights that are used to wrap Christmas trees at Christmas-time. They are made not to get hot and even after hours and days after being placed and lit between the balloons, no balloons should pop or be affected. Also by simply changing a special bulb onto your lighting which is usually included in the lighting set, you can make the lighting of the name or number flash off and on. A stunning effect in low lit restaurants.

When you go looking for your electric air inflator some distributors carry also a continuous flow heavy metal type of air inflator which is purported to be superior to the Qualatex electric air pump. This heavy duty air inflator is about $60 more expensive, much noisier, and heats up at the tip much faster. It has a long extended spout, reminding you a little of a vertical tea pot and has the tendency to tip over and fall on its side by barely touching it.

If you have trouble finding a Qualatex distributor who is willing to carry a wide variety of 5" balloons, you may order them through:

Conwin Carbonic Co.
4510 Sperry Street
Los Angeles, California 90039
(213) 245-2842

Chapter Ten

DOING FLOATING NUMBERS AND LETTERS (without Wire Or PVC)

There are basically two sizes to do letters or numbers. These two sizes are using 5" helixes and 9" helixes. A number "6" done with 5 inch helixes would measure about 3 1/2 feet high. A number "6" done with 9 inch helixes would measure about 8 feet high and if done with helium would have the dramatic property of being able to float. In writing a chapter on floating numbers, we are necessarily talking about *helium* filled 9" helixes. Letters and numbers done with 9" helixes can of course be done with air, internally supported by a very bendable type of thin metal structure called PVC, and hung from a ceiling or some overhead structure. There are advantages *and* disadvantages of both types of letter/number formation. Done with air and using the PVC wiring to form the letters, you have lettering that will last for many days and maybe weeks. The drawback is that if you have to set this lettering up in an auditorium or convention center that has a super high ceiling, you have sometimes some complicated and even dangerous engineering to make it up to the top, place a hook attachment and hang it. This type of letter/number construction is ideal if the event must last several days or weeks.

If the event is a one night affair and you are dealing with a very high ceiling then doing floating numbers and letters *without* PVC is the only way to fly. We particularly enjoy talking about the how-to of doing *floating* numbers and letters because without having anyone available to teach us, we perfected this technique through trial and error. Two samples of floating-number designs done by Balloons by Prosper are the New Year's "1986" design and the number "13" bar-mitzvah design.

Floating Number Designs

As with Chapter 9 - Techniques Of The 5-Inch Balloon, a complete book-length treatise is needed on the detailed explanation of the proper formation of each letter A to Z and each number 1 to 10. But let me give you the *basic* principles and procedures of doing floating numbers or letters. Let us assume that you would like to do a floating "16" for a sweet sixteen celebration. You must first know the number of helixes that you need for each number that you must do which brings me to a very important point: Keep a file record of helix number for every letter, number, or logo that you ever do. If it is a new design formation, you may have to guest at the number of helixes the first time adding or removing a few wherever needed. But as soon as you see the proper number of helixes, record it. To make it easy on you, the "1" contains 13 helixes and the "6" contains 25 helixes. Thirteen plus 25 helixes is 38 helixes times 5 balloons totals 190 balloons. For the total work involved in doing the floating "16", I would charge a flat $250. Remember with some decorations, you can charge a dollar per balloon rate such as in the single arches, but other decorations have to be charged by what you know the job is worth.

Knowing your necessary helix number, you do an outstretched weave as you learned in chapter 7. If you are attempting to form the "6", two people will stand at each extreme of the weave and each person will grab onto the remaining end of the twine and cut it loose from its respective attachments. These two workers then bring this weave down onto a smooth clean floor holding it there momentarily. One of the two workers moves up to the middle of the weave and holds his or her hands gently on top of the weave keeping it down to the floor. You then grab the end of the weave at the position of the person who is now in the middle. While the other two persons hold it down at the other end and the middle, you now smoothly and quickly slide your end of the weave around and inward forming your "6". As you move, you are in a bent over squatted down position. You move bent down in a sort of "duck walk". You now tie your end securely in between helixes and around the middle. You have your "6" formed. Two separate pieces of 50 lb. fishline are tied around the inner curve of the "6" while it is still flat on the floor. These two pieces of fish line are tied two feet apart and are then tied to two brick bases. You now give the signal to release the upper part of the "6" while someone is holding it to the ground by the fish line tied at the two brick bases. The "6" is *raised* to its desired height and tied onto two foil wrapped concrete bricks. The "1" is formed by simply tying the same piece of 50 lb. fish line onto the bottom portion of the upright "1", raising it to the desired level and also tying it onto a foil wrapped concrete brick. This is a sample basic procedure for doing any floating letter or number. One more thing, I recommend floating numbers and letters for *inside decorating only*. On the outside, a strong and sudden gust of wind can suddenly and unexpectedly cause a very costly balloon release.

Chapter 11

DOING BALLOON FLOWERS

One day we were decorating on the outside doing a spiral rainbow weave. To my dismay, I discovered that we had forgotten to double-check on the proper number of balloons that were needed to complete the weave. We got to the last helix of the weave and there were no more colors left. I then told Estela "Put on a helix of all clear, since it's the last one". When she did, something happened. The way the sun hit it, or maybe the angle from which I saw this final helix in place caused me to suddenly cry out, "This looks like the outstretched petals of a *flower!*" A new idea was born. I went home that evening with my head swimming with creative ideas that I eagerly began to experiment.

The first flower design that I did was the Poinsettia Balloon Flowers. It was Christmas-time. The Poinsettia Balloon Flowers consist of two 9" helixes of five balloons per helix, one on top of the other. The bottom helix is all green and the top helix is all ruby red. On top of the ruby red helix is a miniature 5" helix of five citrine yellow balloons. The bottom all green helix represents the green leaves. The all red balloons represent the red poinsettia petals, and the top all yellow 5" balloons conceptualizes the yellow tips seen in the middle-inner portion of the poinsettia plant. The balloon flowers are typically put together in groups of three and sometimes four "flowers". Tule net material or 1 inch thick satin ribbon is then twisted to form "stems" and placed under the bottom portion of each balloon flower and then are tied and connected toward the bottom of the entire "flower set".

The variations of balloon flowers are endless, and this too could be a book in itself. The way that I go about designing balloon flowers is to study *real* flowers or realistically done silk flowers. Nature is always first when it comes to creative ideas. After understanding the basic construction of the Balloon Poinsettias, by simply changing the red balloons to *white*, maintaining the bottom green helix and the top miniature yellow helix the same, I created a concept of *Balloon Daisies*. For a further creative twist, by using water soluble acrylic paint and an artist's brush found at any art supply store, you can stroke on the color markings of different kinds of flowers.

There are basically two types of Balloon Flowers: the air-filled *wall* flowers and the helium-filled *floating* flowers. Though it can be done both ways, the wall flowers are more stable and longer lasting offering you the creative possibility of being able to hand stroke them with paint the night before.

In this chapter, we will go into the how-to of doing the air-filled wall flowers which also follows the basic construction procedures of *helium*-filled balloon flowers.

Get your electric air inflator, 9" balloons, net tule material, paper clips, 10 lb. fish line (to hang them), and small nails or tacks. We will construct a set of balloon daisies like those seen in the following illustration.

Balloon Daisies

The secret to doing a balloon flower is to place *all 10* nine inch balloons *on one paper clip*! To do a balloon daisey, blow up five 9" standard green balloons and five 9" white balloons with your electric air inflator. In the same way that you attach 5 balloons onto a paper clip, attach 5 more onto the same paper clip so that now you have *10 balloons on one paper clip.* At this point, it will look somewhat like a balloon "ball", or sphere of many balloons bunched together. Twist one balloon around another just a few times in the same way that you would do were there an outstretched twine in the middle. Take this balloon ball and flatten it out against a wall making sure that the 5 green balloons form the bottom helix and the 5 white balloons form the "petals". With these first two helixes in place, blow up five miniature-sized 5" citrine yellow balloons and attach them together on a different paper clip. Before closing up this 5" balloon helix, attach the open end of this paper clip onto the paper clip holding the 9" balloons together. Spread them out into their proper places atop the five white 9" inch baloons to form the yellow balloon "pollen". Do two more balloon flowers in this same fashion, and you have a *three-flower set.* Take a piece of your 10 lb. fish line and wrap it in between the two 9" helixes, make a small loop at the top of the fish line and hang it onto a small nail or tack that you have previously placed into the wall. Hang all three flowers in this fashion. Attach tule net or thick satin ribbon on the wall extending from the bottom portion of your three balloon flowers. Group the tule net or satin ribbon together below your set and *voila*-Balloon Daisies. For a visual look at these steps see illustration.

Pricing Balloon Flowers

For a set of a simple balloon flower design that requires no hand painting such as Balloon Daisies or Balloon Poinsettias, I'll charge about $75 per set of 3 flowers. If I do any touching up or hand painting, I'll charge around $95. Your charge includes the concept, the artistry and the time it takes you to set it up.

Balloon flowers can be hung on walls near the cake table of a wedding, anniversary, sweet sixteen, or bar-mitzvah. We once even decorated the walls of a small church *completely covered* with a rainbow of breath-taking balloon flowers.

Doing Balloon Flowers
Step 1

Doing Balloon Flowers
Step 2

Doing Balloon Flowers
Step 3

Chapter 12
DOING BALLOON PEOPLE

Probably one of my greatest brainstorms and contributions to the profession of balloon artistry are the Balloon People.

One evening in November of 1985 I could feel the workings of my creative energies stirring up in the forebrain of my cerebral cortex. I began to see vague images of Christmas-time. They were cartoon like at first then suddenly they became balloon sculptures: candy-canes, snowflakes, and snowmen! "Wow!" I said to myself, "I've got it!" The Snowmen were the first of the family of balloon people, then followed the Clown, the Tuxedo men, and the fabulous Bride and Groom. For a cameo appearance of all these famous characters together for the first time, see the illustrations which follow.

The Balloon People
(The Snowmen & Clowns)

118

The Balloon People
(The Tuxedo Men & The Bride & Groom)

119

The Snowmen

The snowmen design is typically a design of Christmas-time that is usually done in conjunction with a pair of balloon candy canes. The balloon candy canes are done by doing a helium-filled red and white 9" five-balloon helix spiral using a helix formula of 2 ruby red and 3 white balloons. Do about 30 helixes. Tie a piece of 40 lb. fish line on the top of one end of this weave after it is finished. Place it on the floor. Holding the fish line, bend it inward forming the cane and tie it around the upper body of the weave. Tie a foil wrapped brick on the opposite end of the cane which will be the base where it sits on the floor. When released to stand upright there is a tendency for a helium-filled balloon candy cane to bend backward. To control this backward movement, another piece of fish line is tied around the middle portion of the point where the cane curves and is run down to the floor where it is tied to another foil wrapped brick. Now you have a well-formed and stationary balloon candy cane.

The construction of the snowmen is the simplest yet nonetheless one of the most effective of the Balloon People variations. The key element to doing all of the balloon people is to *use air instead of helium*. They will last for weeks. Start your snowman by weaving six white helixes of 5 balloons per helix. The balloons are the usual 9" balloons used in all standard weaves. After your six all white helixes are finished and woven into place, cut the twine at both ends to remove this short weave from its outstretched horizontal position. On to one end, tie a foil wrapped brick to serve as the base. Once in upright position, take your electric inflator and blow up a white 16" balloon to form the head. Using a jumbo size paper clip, attach it to the inner lip of the knot-tip of the inflated 16" balloon "head". Attach the head onto the top helix at its clip. Blow up very small two black 5" balloons and one ruby red 5" balloon. Tie them and cut off the lip tip above the little knots. Using double stick transparent tape, tape the black eyes and the red nose into position. Wrap a five-foot green cloth scarf around the neck. You now take a black top hat, and with very small scissors like those used by cosmetologists for cutting nails, perforate a tiny hole on opposite sides of the brim. The purpose of this is to insert a piece of 20 lb. fish line into each hole and make a knot at the top of each hole so that it can't be pulled through. Holding onto about 4 inches of fish line on each side of the bottom portion of the brim, tape the top hat securely onto both sides of the balloon head so that it won't fall off in the course of the evening.

(Top hats and green cloth scarfs can be ordered through the Balloons by Prosper wholesale department. See Appendix). For a step-by-step visual look at the construction of a Balloon Snowman, see illustration.

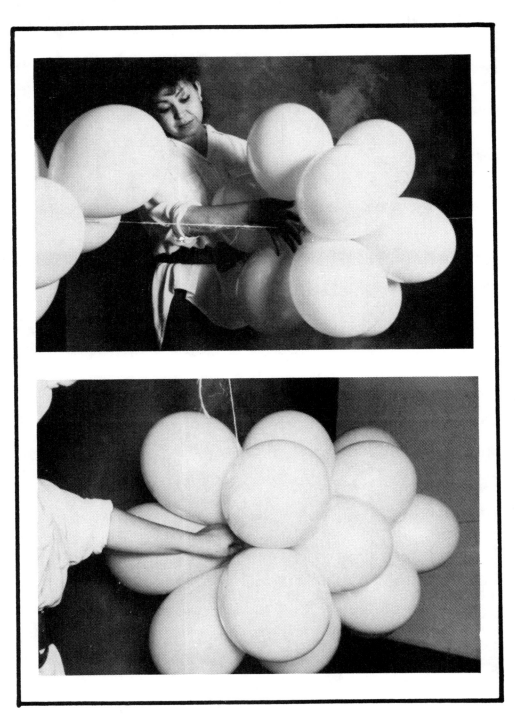

Doing Balloon Snowmen
a) Pushing Helixes in Place
b) End Tying

Doing Balloon Snowmen
(Tying on Brick Base)

123

Doing Balloon Snowmen
(Clipping on the Head)

124

Doing Balloon Snowmen
(Final Touches)

As with all balloon people, we suggest that they be *sold in pairs*. One balloon person standing by itself doesn't really create much of an impact. As for pricing, I usually charge $90 a pair for the snowmen.

The Clowns

If you remember that with the snowmen, we used 6 sections (or helixes) with 5 balloons per section. The clown, the tuxedo men, and the bride and groom follow a different pattern of rules: You use *7 sections* (or helixes) and each section has *6 balloons* per clip. Sixteen inch heads are used, but a 5" balloon helix of six balloons is placed around the base of the 16" balloon head forming a type of collar which lifts up the balloon head slightly giving it the appearance of a neck. The clown and all other balloon people are *always done with air* and are attached at the bottom to a foil wrapped concrete brick.

To do the clown, start out by air inflating six 9" balloons in rainbow colors: 1 ruby red, 1 orange, 1 citrine yellow, 1 green, 1 sapphire blue, and 1 quartz purple. Attach these six balloons onto a standard paper clip. This is your first helix. Do six more helixes in the same way. Attach all 7 helixes onto your outstretched twine. Starting with your first helix, twist two or three balloons a few times around your twine until it is snug and secure but not too tight. To spread open a six-balloon helix, you will need an assistant to stand behind this first helix and have his or her stomach and chest serve as a "wall" on which to flatten out this helix. He or she stands there until you have twisted and pushed into place at least three initial helixes. The helixes should now stay in place by themselves. There is a certain helix color pattern that you must follow. To arrange in proper order this rainbow helix of six balloons, start with the ruby red and move clockwise. You will have ruby red, followed by orange, then yellow, then green, then blue, and finally purple to complete the color circle. To do the color swirl or spiral, twist according to standard procedure. Rotate each helix into position by following the clockwise movement of the red balloon. Every time you push a helix into place, you rotate it one balloon to the right. After seven rotations, you will have a very attractive rainbow swirl.

Upon completing your seventh section, cut the weave from its vertical position. Using about 2 feet of remaining twine from the ends of the weave, tie your end and tie on securely your foil wrapped concrete brick. You may now place your "headless" clown into a vertical position.

Blow up your 16" white head and tie a knot. Take a jumbo paper clip and hook it into the inner lip tip just below the knot of your balloon head. Blow up six 5" clear balloons and clip them together using a standard size paper clip. This is your clown "collar" but at the same time it has the functional use of lifting up slightly the head to give the clown the appearance of having a neck. Without this "neck" the balloon head squats grotesquely into the center of the weave. Insert the jumbo clip holding the 16" head into the center of the 5" clear helix collar. With this head-and-collar combo, hook the jumbo clip into the middle of the top helix of your headless weave at the point where all six balloons are attached together to the paper clip. Blow up twenty-four citrine yellow 5" balloons about one inch in diameter and cutoff the balloon tip below the knot using scissors or the razor edge of your helium valve. Put all of your 5" balloons in a cardboard box. Blow up a ruby red 5" balloon about two inches in diameter and cut off the tip. Take seven more 5" ruby red balloons and blow this up as small as possible, again cutting off the tips. Blow up two sapphire blue 5" balloons one inch in diameter, knot and cut off the tips.

As you look into the cardboard box, you will see the various sizes and colors of your inflated 5" balloons. Within this box lies the eyes, nose, mouth, and hair of your rainbow Balloon Clown. With a roll of transparent double-stick tape found at any stationery store, you begin the face. Take the two blue balloons and attach them into the position of the eyes. The one-inch diameter ruby red balloon is taped between the two eyes and just about two inches below into the position of the nose. With white acrylic paint or even a bottle of "white-out" correction fluid paint a large white dot on the nose. Take the seven mini ruby red balloon and tape a smile. With the twenty-four yellow balloons, tape twelve on each side of the head to form the "hair", pressing them tightly together. You may also blow up more yellow balloons and run them around the back of the head keeping him bald at the top. After finishing your "balloon cosmetology", Curly the Clown (as we call him), is ready for his clown hat. A red hat is recommended though any of the six rainbow colors will work. (Clown hats may be obtained through the Balloons by Prosper wholesale list. See Appendix).

As with attaching the top hat onto the balloon snowman, make a small hole into opposite sides of the clown hat brim using a very small and pointed pair of scissors. Insert a piece of 20 lb. fish line into each hole and make a knot at the top. With about four inches of fish line extending from the bottom, tape the clown hat on each side of the white head. *Voila.* You have an official rainbow swirl Balloon Clown.

Remember all Balloon People are done and sold in pairs. A pair of Balloon Clowns are sold for $150.00 plus tax.

Doing the Balloon Clowns
(Placing Helixes)

129

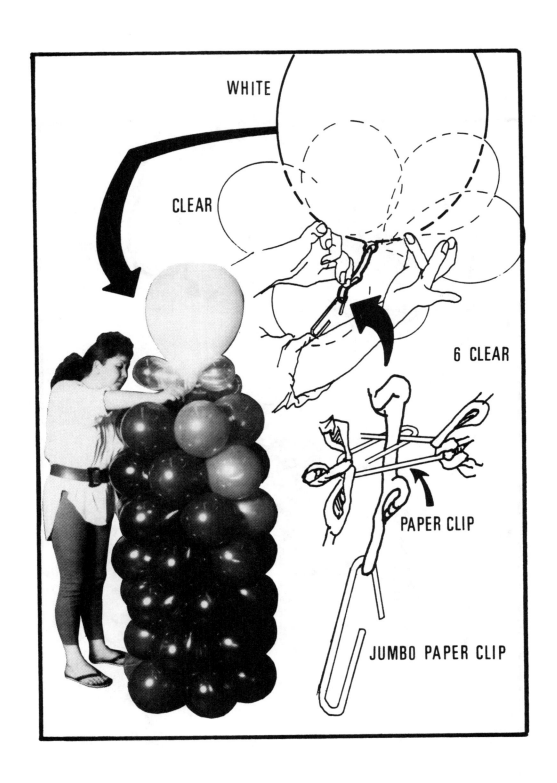

WHITE

CLEAR

6 CLEAR

PAPER CLIP

JUMBO PAPER CLIP

**Doing the Balloon Clowns
(Clipping on the Head)**

130

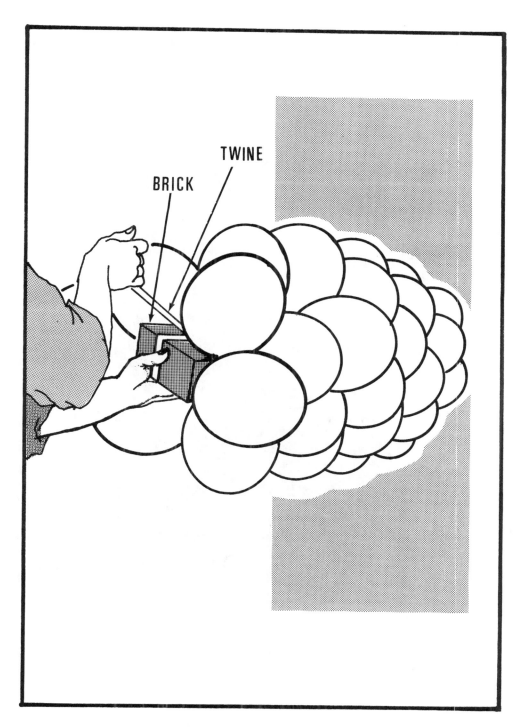

TWINE

BRICK

Doing the Balloon Clowns
(Tying on Brick Base)

131

Doing the Balloon Clowns
(Final Touches)

The Tuxedo Men

One of my greatest brainstorms and without hesitation the pride and joy of my design portfolio are the Tuxedo Men. Their construction follows the basic steps that we saw with the clown. Seven helixes are used of 9" balloons of *six* balloons per helix. A six-balloon helix of 5" *clear* balloons is used as a collar to proudly lift the 16" clear head which is crowned with a top hat. A foil-wrapped concrete brick serves as the base.

After attaching the mandatory twine to the doorknobs of two opposite sides of the room, air inflate 4 all black helixes of six balloons per helix using standard size paper clips. Twist your 4 all black helixes into place which will form the black "pants" of the tux-look. With your first 4 helixes woven securely into place, blow up 3 all metallic silver helixes of six balloons per helix. Weave these three helixes into place. Cut the twine ends from off the doorknobs. Tie your ends and take your foil-wrapped concrete brick and tie it securely to the base of the black sections. You may now stand up your headless tuxedo man and prepare for the final steps. Blow up six 5" clear balloons and attach them to a standard size paper clip. This is your "collar" helix. Blow up a 16" clear balloon, tie it and attach one jumbo clip at the bottom tip into the inner lip just below the knot. Insert this jumbo clip holding the 16" clear head into the middle of the 5" clear "collar" helix. With this head and collar combination, attach the jumbo clip to the middle inner portion of the top all-silver helix just at the point where all six silver balloons meet at the paper clip. Arrange the collar into place and tie around it a Balloons by Prosper custom-made black bow tie (obtainable from our wholesale list). Tape on your black top hat as was done with the Snowmen; do one more Tuxedo Man to make a pair, and you have a classic balloon design. The Tuxedo Men should be sold for *at least* $150 per pair.

The Bride And Groom

A step further in the design concept of the Tuxedo Men is the Bride and Groom. To make things simple, the Groom is done exactly as the Tuxedo Man: black balloon trousers, metallic silver shirt, black bow tie and black top hat. (Stay away from innovative changes such as pastel tuxs, pink trousers, white top hats and the like. We don't want any "fruity" grooms).

The Bride is done with the most elegant simplicity - *7 helixes of all white balloons* of six balloons per helix. The 5" balloon helix collar is done with six *5" metallic silver balloons* which serves to lift the 16" clear head but at the same time gives the appearance of a *pearl necklace*. A foil-wrapped concrete brick is attached to the bottom of the weave after tying your ends by securely wrapping it with the remaining twine. Now in her upright position, the Bride is ready to be crowned with a custom-made white veil also obtainable from the Balloons by Prosper wholesale list. See Appendix.

For heaven's sake, resist the temptation to put on a balloon face, or as someone suggested to me, balloon "lips" so that the balloon Bride and Groom can face each other and kiss. This is a work of *elegance*, imagination, and sophistication. You are to *imagine* the face of the Bride and Groom. Once you start haphazardly attaching appendages where there should be none, you will soon find yourself putting on balloon arms, a balloon buttocks, and a balloon "something-else" that I don't even want to mention. Why are you smiling?

The Bride and Groom should sell for at least $150.00 and it is a "must" design concept to offer to all of your wedding clients.

Chapter 13
TECHNIQUES OF CREATIVE THINKING—HOW IDEAS COME

Techniques of Creative Thinking is a chapter that could easily merit an entire book treatise, but there are certain basic principals and techniques that I can lay out for you that can give you a tremendous headstart in becoming a creative designer. Let me say something that I have said numerous times in my decoration seminars that I would like to repeat for your benefit now. More and more people will get into this exciting profession of balloon decorating, but the ones who will eventually stand out amongst the rest are those who constantly strive to come up with more and more innovative designs. The most creative balloon design has not been done yet, and never will be, for creativity is a *process* on a ever continuing journey toward perfection. It is unfortunate that the history of this business has been riddled by envy and plagarism where the name of the game has been "steal the idea and take the credit". But those who steal ideas the most while taking all of the credit and sharing what they have learned the least are only demonstrating the unspoken faith in their own ineptitude. A creative mind does not flourish with disuse. We are here on this earth to share our creative gifts *collectively* with the entire family of man. The more we give of ourselves, the more we give *to* ourselves. This another way of saying that God gives to the giver and takes from the taker. Let us be plentiful with the gifts of our spirit.

What Is Genius

Simply put, genius is learning how to use more of your mind and to use it in a special way. The special way is to produce creative ideas at will. It has been said by many noted experts in the field of psychology and brain physiology that most of us are using only 1/10 of our mental capacities with a vast 90% of our mental capabilities

135

being left as vast unused fertile wasteland, something like going about out daily lives using only the little finger of the left hand while ignoring the combined power of the ten fingers of both hands.

In this chapter, I will show you how to use more of your mind and how to use it in a special way - to produce creative ideas at will.

Left Brain/Right Brain Thinking

One of the most important discoveries in recent years on the total functioning of the human brain is the understanding of left and right brain thinking. From an early age while at school all the way up to and through adulthood, we have been conditioned almost exclusively to employ left brain type of thinking versus *right brain* thinking. Let me elaborate. If you look at a human brain, you will notice that there is a big cleavage right down the middle separating the brain into two hemispheres-a right hemisphere and a left hemisphere. Left brain thinking is logical and analytical while right brain thinking is *imaginative* and *creative*. The right brain is also most active when we sleep and dream. All throughout school, we have been admonished "to wake up and stop daydreaming". But ironically, it is in this imaginative, daydreaming state that out greatest creative treasures can be found. The goal is not to ignore left brain logical thinking but to integrate and utilize the left and right brain hemisphere to allow *whole* - brain thinking - the "stuff" of which *geniuses* are made.

Techniques Of Creative Thinking

Our purpose is to find the *quickest* and most efficient techniques for producing money-making creative ideas by learning how to tap into this infinite resource of our *right brain* hemisphere. The key to this is a technique called *creative visualization* which if you practice daily for at least 21 days, you will see a marked difference in your creative ability.

For fifteen minutes before you go to bed and fifteen minutes after you wake up in the morning, I want you to prop yourself up in the bed. Turn off the TV, radio, stereo, silence the telephone, and make it very clear to your family that you are not to be disturbed during these most important 15 minutes. Count backwards slowly from 25 to 1 relaxing your entire body with each retrogressive count more and more. You are to visualize yourself in your office or some other room familiar to you, and imagine that you are standing in front of and talking with Michaelangelo, Leonardo Da Vinci, Rodin or any other famous artist or sculptor living or dead. Whomever you choose to be your imaginary "mental counselor", mentally see yourself greeting him or her and see him or her responding in turn. This is the technique: Let us say that you are working on a new design concept for a client who has a Christmas theme. You simply pose a question like "Mr. Da Vinci, what are some possible design concepts for Christmas using balloons?" The first thought that pops into your mind is your imaginary counselor's answer. In the beginning it will feel as though you are "making these answers up". This is the right feeling. Three things you will find as you practice this obstensibly silly technique: 1) These imaginary answers will come faster and better each time; 2) Ideas will pop into your head when you least expect it all throughout the day. (So always keep a pad and pencil on hand with you). 3) When you practice this visualization just before you go to sleep, you will increasingly have and remember dreams that will give you rich creative ideas. Be not surprised that when you wake, your head will be pregnant with really great creative concepts ready for execution.

To understand and get more into the techniques of creative visualization for triggering creative solutions to your toughest problems. I *highly* recommend the book: *The Silva Mind Control Method For Business Managers* by Jose Silva published by Pocket Books of New York and obtainable in paperback for only $3.95 at all major bookstores. This is must-reading.

Part II

HOW TO MAKE UP TO $100,000 A YEAR IN YOUR OWN DECORATING BUSINESS

Chapter 14

OPERATING FROM HOME VS. OPERATING FROM A STORE FRONT

In setting up shop for your exciting new balloon decoration business, you may do it in one of two ways: You may operate from home or you may operate from a store front.

Operating from Home

Let me set the records straight. You can work successfully from your home or apartment, develop a professional image, and make lots and lots of money. I worked successfully from an apartment averaged $500 to $1000 per week just working weekends doing wedding and large party decorations. There is a certain art and science of working from a home or apartment. Certain aspects of this operation must be carefully worked out.

Your living room is important. You are working at a slight disadvantage to the person who has a store. Your competitor who has a store *appears* to be more stable and professional for no other reason than he or she is in the constant view of the public eye. A person working from home or an apartment theoretically can receive a large deposit on a decoration, skip town, and "blow" all of the money in a carefree spree in Las Vegas. To couteract any doubts or fears on the part of clients that come to your home or apartment to see you is to create and maintain a professional image of your *living room* at all times. You are to create an office out of your living room. This means *remove* any TV, stereo, tricycle, baby's play pen, or *baby himself* from view. None of your kids will be allowed to play in this room at any time. Indoor plants like tall palms and ficus benjamina trees are recommended decor for corners of the room. A desk and chair in the middle of the room is mandatory. On a magazine table be sure that you have copies of magazines such as *Souvenir* to keep their minds on *balloons*. Soft FM "elevator music" is permissible. But the most important key to creating the image you want to portray is *you* and how you dress. Though it may be your house or apartment, you are always to receive your clients with a three piece business suit if you are a man or a woman's business outfit if you are a lady. This is *most* important. Don't give way to the

141

temptation to see your clients with your favorite T-shirt, jeans, and tennis. If you were an executive working for someone else, you wouldn't dress like this. Why not give *yourself* the same prestige?

If your living room leads visibly to the kitchen, bedroom or some other room that distracts from the business-like aura you are trying to create, get a folding portable wall, or put up a curtain to block off the view of the other room. Nothing should stand in your way of immersing your clients in a complete office ambience. I can remember many times when big important corporate executives would go to my apartment to see my portfolio and ask "Do you live here also?"

Be careful how you refer to your apartment *number* when you are setting up appointments on the phone. Instead of saying "I'm in apartment 77," you say suite 77 or room 77. Once they arrive, they'll still knock on the door and upon entering see you in your *office*.

If you happen to be male, care must be taken to set up appointments for females to come and see portfolios at your apartment. Sometimes it is good to allow your wife or girlfriend to set the appointment just to put a prospective female client at ease by hearing another female voice.

Be sure to have an answering machine especially the type with remote control that allows you to call from outside every couple hours to check your messages. And see your decoration clients *by appointment only.* You don't want any important clients to knock on your door at 8:00 A.M. and catch you with your pajamas on. Don't even answer your door if you are not prepared and properly dressed. If friends must come up and visit you, ask them to *call* before dropping by. This is your place of *business.*

Operating from a Store Front

The first thing that I want to say about operating from a store front is that you really don't *need* any more than 800 square feet to get started. Being in the public eye, you will automatically attract foot traffic and new customers. If you select your locale carefully in a prospering and upwardly mobile neighborhood, your clients should steadily grow more and more each year.

Store Window is Important

The thing that will most establish your image and reputation as a top-notched decorator is your store window. It is here that people will get their first impression of how good you are. Doing any combination of the Balloon People in your store window with a set of daily replenished King-7's is always a sure winner. In searching for a nice store front, try to get one that has a nice picture view window *on the shady side of the street.*

Negotiate a short lease of say 1 year to start to see how you like it and following the first successful year, negotiate a longer and longer lease on the date of each renewal.

The initial starting capital from an in-home operation can be as little as $500 with the average start-up capital, including necessary inventory, for a storefront is about $7000. In your store, you will sell mylars, stuffed-animal gifts, and balloon arrangements to your *walk-in* customers. You will find delivery requests ever increasing the longer you are at your locale and the better known you become. Retail sales and decoration contracts can become very, very lucrative business. I grossed $6000 per month after only the first two months of opening my store. Part of this success of course was that I layed the groundwork, building up a clientele by *first* working from home.

Chapter 15

STARTING YOUR
DECORATION PHOTO ALBUM

Although I have been successfully doing this business for more than 8 years and have many winning design concepts to offer, I have yet to be able to effectively convince a prospective customer on the basis of a *verbal description* only. In other words, you need a full-color decoration portfolio to *show* what you do. Many, many people are still totally unaware of all of the creative design possibilities that can be done with balloons. I would make an educated guess than more than 50% of the population has never seen a real live balloon weave traversing proudly from one side of a main table to the other. You can *explain* it, but they still won't *see* it.

An impressive and professional looking decoration portfolio consists of 8" x 10" color prints and the most expensive looking photo album that you can get your hands on. I suggest that the album cover be dark brown with a wood type finish, with gilded edges as a final touch. The album should be such that the pages turn easily. You will have some clients who like to flip the pages at *warp-speed*. Have a friend who is a professional wedding photographer order for you one of his or her fanciest and richest looking albums that *they* use to showcase their wedding photography.

Hire Someone to Take Your Photos

Unless you are a professional photographer yourself, it is worth every penny invested to hire someone to take quality photos of your decorations. When I say that you should hire someone, I don't mean that you should hire the most well-known studio photographer in your city but rather a reliable *freelance* photographer who works from home or part-time and will charge you no more than $40.00 to go out and do and on-site shooting of your decoration. Your photographer should use 35 millimeter color film and never 110 film used for pocket instamatics. Thirty-five millimeter film is the film size you'll need to make quality color enlargements. The arrangement that you should make with your photographer is that he or she will take a 24 exposure role of your decoration and give *you* the film to develop. This is very important because you want to eternally have control over your negatives. After my photographer finishes a shooting, I take the roll of film and I rush over to one of the One-Hour film processing places here in Los Angeles and see how my prints come out on the *same day.*

Let me give you a tip about taking *really* good decoration photos that will impress your prospective clients with the greatest of ease: Take your photographs *before* the guests arrive, *with no people in the picture.* A decoration photo with no people mulling around in tuxedos and evening gowns allows the quiet beauty of your design to step forth. Put a bald-headed man with a cigar in the middle and you've ruined it. Remember your photo album is your bread and butter. It is literally *your most important sales tool.* If it is done well enough with the most beautiful designs available, you won't need to worry too much about *what* to say. Your album *will speak for itself.*

Using Someone Else's Photos

To my knowledge, there are only three major companies (including my own) that give seminars on the how-to of doing balloon decorations. It is the practice of all three of us to sell 8"x10" color photos for students to allow them a quick and easy way to build their portfolio. Well intentioned as this may be, there can be some very serious drawbacks to the misuse of this portfolio building availability. Don't state to a prospective client that *you* did the decoration if you didn't. Let me illustrate an amusing happenstance here in Los Angeles. Four fairly well established balloon companies happened to take one of the other two balloon decoration seminars that I mention above. Well, these four balloon companies happened to *each* buy *all of the same photos* sold after this particular decoration seminar. They each put the *same* photos in their decoration portfolio and they *all* claimed to be the originators of the decorations. I discovered this by accident because a bewildered client came into my office and said,"My goodness, you are the first balloon company I have visited today that doesn't have the *exact same photos in their portfolio.*" The purpose and *only* purpose of using any photo that does not happen to be yours is to be able to show a client the *types* of things that you *can* do with balloons and what you are *able* to do for him. The minute you sell a decoration, hire a photographer and take *your own photos.* Then you can proudly and truthfully say this is *my* work. There is something about a photo when it is a decoration actually done by you. You speak with confidence and authority because you are speaking through *experience.* Once you have your own photo, the initial photo has served its purpose and it should be filed away in your nearest desk drawer. You are on your way to building a first class money-making portfolio.

Chapter 16
SPECIALIZE IN WEDDINGS

You can do balloon artistry for grand openings, birthdays, bar-mitzvahs, Christmas and New Years parties, but the most consistent, lucrative, and stable way to make a living in the balloon decoration profession is to specialize in *weddings*. As mentioned earlier, we average as many as 5 weddings every weekend. And this is the beauty of wedding decorating especially if you operate from home and have a full-time job: it is *Saturday-only decorating*. Most wedding decorations if done skillfully and with taste will average about $300 each sometimes going as high as $500, $600, or more.

Avoid Ceiling Cascades

The novice in decorating or the client who is trying to take control usually suggest the use of ceiling cascades. Ceiling cascades are basically bouquets of helium-filled balloons with long curling ribbon that are released and are allowed to hang from the ceiling causing a very colorful and eye-catching cascade effect. Whenever we do ceiling cascades, we like to do them with the silver mylar ribbon which gives it an exciting and dazzling tinsel look. The only problem with doing ceiling cascades is that for most reception halls that will hold an average of 250 people, you have to use *hundreds and hundreds* of 11" balloons to *properly* cover the ceiling. What this means to your customer is that he or she will wind up having almost all of their decoration budget go up on the ceiling. Ceiling cascades work well in small rooms such as an average living room or in a small enclosed ceiling like the type over certain dance areas. The balloons cover an area without rolling from one corner of the room to the other.

Scheduling is Important

In order to be able to successfully handle 3,4,or 5 wedding decorations in one day, you must be a master of scheduling. You must know approximately how long each decoration will take, how far you must travel form one decoration to the next, the time the guests are supposed to arrive,and the time the hall is available for you to go in and decorate. Let me make something very clear. A schedule is always *written*. A typical schedule that you might follow on Saturday might look like the following illustration.

CLIENT	DECORATION	HOURS TO DO	WHERE	HALL AVAILABLE	WE ARRIVE	WE LEAVE	GUESTS ARRIVE	COMMENT
1. CATHY CASTRO	• 1. WEAVE • 1. KING-7 SET • 20 TABLES WITH CANDLE BASE BOUQUETS	2 HOURS	LONG BEACH	10:00 A.M.	9:45 A.M.	12:00 NOON	2:00 P.M.	
2. THELMA DAY	• 1. FLOATING HEART • 2. CLEAR BOUQUETS • 25 TABLES WITH CHAMAY BOTTLES BASE AND BOUQUETS	2½ HOURS	LOS ANGELES	11:00 A.M.	1:00 P.M.	3:30 P.M.	5:00 P.M.	
3. MARTIN PAYTON	• 1. BRIDE AND GROOM • 1. KING-7 SET	45 MIN.	SANTA MONICA	1:00 P.M.	4:00 P.M.	5:00 P.M.	6:00 P.M.	
4. SUSAN BROWN	• 1. WEAVE • 1. KING-7 SET	45 MIN.	SANTA MONICA	2:00 P.M.	5:30 P.M.	6:30 P.M.	7:00 P.M.	
5. SERGIO TORRES	• 1. BRIDE AND GROOM	30 MIN.	LOS ANGELES	3:00 P.M.	7:00 P.M.	7:30 P.M.	8:00 P.M.	

Decoration Schedule Card

To relieve a lot of unnecessary stress on you, arrange for your clients to *pay out in full* any time *before* the day of the decoration. It has been our misfortune on numerous occasions to arrive at the specified time, finish the decoration and have to *wait* for a client 30 to 45 minutes *late* with the balance. This causes you to be thrown off schedule for the *next* decoration.

We have developed the ability to do many decorations in one day by inflating balloons and clipping on helixes in our vans while on route from on decoration to another. It is an amazing sight to see our trained and highly skilled workers sitting on their pillows while inflating and clipping together all of the necessary helixes. A helium tank will lie flat with a valve pointing upward. Most times we'll stop at a small sandwich shop to eat, but many times we'll rotate: eating, resting, working, and driving-*all within the confines of the van and all done while in route to the next decoration.*

Chapter 17

HOW TO GET
DECORATION CONTRACTS

It is very interesting that with all of the excitement of learning how to do balloon artistry and decorations that most people overlook that fact doing first-class balloon decorations is only *half* of the formula to becoming successful. Knowing how to market your skills and service is the other half.

When most newcomers enter into the balloon decoration business, like it or not, they are unwittingly faced with the inescapable necessity of deciding the most effective and affordable means of getting new business and building a clientele. To teach you how to successfully obtain an almost endless stream of top-notched clients and major corporations, I am going to make an assumption. The assumption I am going to make is that you are starting with little or no starting capital. With a massive advertising budget, matters become simple. You just hire a first-rate advertising agency. They will design your ads and select the appropriate newspapers, magazines, and trade publications in which you should advertise. They will also send you a bill which will sometimes be as much as $2000 or $3000 a month depending on how aggressive that they decide to launch your ad campaign.

I have always held the philosophy that there are two ways to get started in a new business: 1) With a *lot* of capital and little creative ideas, or 2) With little capital and a *lot* of creative ideas. When you are rich in creative ideas, be it for marketing or designing new concepts, money will always find a way to catch up and jump into your pockets. Let me reveal to you the "Prosper Method" of getting new business.

Teleblitzing - The Secret Of Dialing For Dollars

I am always thoroughly amused when I tell my students that the most effective and probably the most inexpensive and accessible marketing tool that they could ever lay their hands on is the *telephone* sitting quietly in front of them everyday. Many go about a daily ritual of scratching their heads and wondering how they are going to bring in more business. Lying within the pages of their city's yellow page directory are probably *hundreds* of companies

151

and organizations that are badly in need of decorations services. They don't know about you, and you don't know about them. But they *are* somewhere in there. So now, it is a question of discovering *who*. Look under Organizations, Clubs, Churches, Sororities, Fraternities, Colleges, and Universities. At some time during the year all organizations, clubs, churches, sororities, fraternities, colleges and universities will hold or stage some major festivity or event. If they find out about you in time, you could land new decoration business before your competition can even move a muscle.

On 3" x 5" plain index cards, write down the name, address, zip code and phone number of each prospect from the various categories listed above. A separate index card is for each prospect. I suggest that you start with a stack of at least 100 prospects that you will systematically call one-by-one at a pre-chosen time of the day-Monday through Friday. Nine a.m. to 12 noon is a good block of time to do your *telebilitzing* as well as 1:00 p.m. to 4:00 p.m. (Most people usually go out for lunch between 12 noon and 1:00 p.m.) The purpose of these calls is to talk to the person in charge of the *decoration aspect* of their special events and festivities. Let us say that you call a certain club from your list. You would say something like:

> "Hello, may I speak to the person who would
> probably be in charge of the decoration aspect
> of your club parties and reunions?"
>
> "Oh, you want to speak with Hilda."
>
> "Hello, Hilda, may I speak to the person who would
> probably be in charge of the decoration aspect of
> your club parties and reunions?"

Hilda-   That's me. How can I help you?

You-   My name is (*your name*) and I am a balloon artist
        specializing in balloon decoration designs done
        especially for special events that your club
        might give. I know you're very busy, and I don't
        want to take much of your time. I would just
        like to arrange 5 minutes to stop by your office
        and show you my portfolio.

At this point she'll either say she's not interested, or "*Can you send me some literature?*" If she says she's not interested, simply say thanks and go on to the next index card. If she requests literature, send her a color snapshot of one of your *best* decorations along with a cover letter containing your letterhead and logo describing your services and experience. Follow up in 5 days with another call to the same person and try to uncover when their next major event is scheduled to be. At this point, you will both know if there is any genuine decoration possibilities for you. If a prospect to whom you are speaking grants you an appointment to go in to show your portfolio on the first call, be assured that this is a very promising sign. A major decoration could be just around the corner. If you make at least 20 phone contacts per day, five days a week, you will be making 100 phone contacts per week or 400 phone contacts per month. You should be able to sell at least 5 decorations per week and none should be less that $250 each. You will eventually have a series of appointments during the week to go out to *show* your portfolio which will of course interrupt your *daily* phone teleblitzing. At this point you should have your husband or wife, sweetheart or business partner continue the daily calls while you go out to show the portfolio and *sell* the decorations.

Follow Your Local Newspaper

Another way to create a profitable prospect list is through your local newspaper. Instead of titillating yourself with sensationalist and useless news of all that's going bad in your town, follow the special events, fairs, conventions and shows. Any organization sponsoring any of the above has an immediate need for special effect decorating which you can provide for them. If it's a convention, you call and use the same procedure as explained above by saying, "May I speak with the person who is probably in charge of the decoration aspect of your convention?" Continue as already instructed.

Creating A Referral Source Network

It has been said that the best source of new business is word-of-mouth, and it is on this principle that I will show you how to create a *referral source network*. From now on anybody, and I mean *anybody*, who refers new business to you, should receive a *thank-you note* and a *check* representing 10% of the total amount that was sold from the decoration. Many people will call and say that you really didn't *have* to send them any money that, they only wanted to *help*. I have yet to receive a *returned* check. You should make a list of caterers, musicians, dee jays, wedding photographers, limousine companies, and wedding cake decorators and go in to their businesses and show them your portfolio. Explain what you do and make them your 10% commission offer on any decoration sold that is referred by them. These are your referral source network. You should set a goal of having at least *100 participants* in this network. When you make this 10% arrangement with members of your active network, give them good sales materials. You should give them some *sample* photos and some business cards. Better yet, give them some full-color *photo* business-cards which are actually business-card-size photographs of your best designs with the name of your business and phone number *printed* on it. These cards are about $250 per 1000 utilizing one of your photos and can be ordered from:

Success Cards Unlimited
2554 Lincoln Blvd. Suite 1001
Marina Del Rey, California 90291
(213) 292-0911

They make an *excellent* sales tool for those who refer business to you.

Placing Business Cards After Decorating

The simplest and most effective way to use regular business cards to get new business is after decorating. In this case, you use *inexpensive* plain white business cards that should run you about $25 per 1000. After you finish a decoration, you take a small handful of your cards and place them in between the salt and pepper shaker on each table. If there are 10 chairs per table, be sure that you place *at least* 10 business cards in between each salt and pepper shaker. The idea is that if there are going to be 500 guests at a given event where you are decorating, you want to be sure that *each* of 500 people will walk out of that hall with one of your business card in their pocket. Just think, in just one evening, 500 people will know about you and carry out your card who didn't know about you before they walked in. Imagine if you did two different events in the same evening and both were hosting 500 guests each. *One thousand people* would know about you for a $25 advertising cost. Wow!

We go through at least 1000 business cards *per week*, sometimes as many as 1500. And contrary to popular opinion, people do *not* mind when you *neatly* leave your business cards on the tables. You will hear the guests walking through the doors and saying "How beautiful! Who *did* the balloons?"

Don't keep your business a secret.

Chapter 18

KEEPING A FILE AND KEEPING IN TOUCH WITH YOUR CUSTOMERS

Don't think that if you start from home and decide to only work part-time weekends that you won't be required to exercise the same type of organization and control that you would were you to have a store. Keeping some type of file system and keeping in touch with your customers *and* members of your referral source network is vitally important. There are many ways to go about this. The simplest method that I have found to file-keeping is to get a stack of 3" x 5" plain white index cards, alphabetical dividers, and a "shoe-box" type file box found at most stationery stores to hold the index cards. For every new customer you make, place his or her last name first followed by a comma then their first name along with the address, city-state-zip, phone number, the date the order was placed, a description of what was delivered or how it was decorated, and most importantly *who* was the referral source. You will also place on this index card the invoice number of the decoration done. (We will talk more about writing decoration invoices in chapter 19 in the discussion on writing a decoration contract). To take a look at how an index card should be written up, see illustration on the following page.

The Index File-Card

You will also have an index card for each of the members of your *referral source network*. But for *these* important resources, I suggest that you put them on *pink* index cards and group them all together with a rubber band. Place them toward the *back* of your file box and behind the white index file-cards used for your customers.

The Importance Of Thank-You Notes

There is a little secret that doesn't cost much, ignored by most, and brings *instant* and *guaranteed* results. The *thank-you note*. You can solidify the loyalty of any client as well as stimulate *tremendous* referral activity by sending every client or new member of your referral source team a thank-you note:

PRESTON, JANICE
1521 ORANGE GROVE
LOS ANGELES, CA. 90019
(213) 449-1123

REFERRED BY ROB'S CATERING
10%

INVOICE #2023
WEDDING MAY 9-87

- 4/2/87 - ORDERED 1. WEAVE / KING - 7 SET WITH 20 TABLE ARRANGEMENTS.
- 4/3/87 - I SENT HER THANK-YOU NOTE
- 4/4/87 - I SENT ROB'S CATERING 10% COMMISSION CHECK OF $47.50

Index File Card

after every appointment, after every sale, and *after every referral*-whether they buy or not. This you must do consistently, religiously, and without fail. I guarantee you *immediate* results. There will be more referrals and more sales. When was the last time *you* received a thank-you note? Imagine how special a customer or referral source member will feel upon receiving an unexpected thank-you note. Now, the key to making this thank-you technique work is that it must be *written* and it must be *sent*. Go to your stationery store and you will find small packs of thank-you notes with envelopes made especially for this purpose. Hallmark Cards puts out a very nice selection. You want to select thank-you cards that have no message inside, so that you can write in a short and personal message like: "Rob, thanks for the opportunity to meet with you - Charles", or "Janice, thank-you for the opportunity to show you my album - Charles", or "David, thanks for the referral - Charles". I think you get the idea.

Now, in your selection of thank-you notes, be sure that the thank-you notes with the flowers and butterflies go to your *female* recipients and the *plainer* looking ones go to your *male* recipients. You don't want to convey the wrong message.

Why do thank-you notes work so well? I'm not sure. But I sort of suspect that *thank*-you is really like *bless*-you. We all like to be *blessed* whether we sneeze or not.

Monthly Greetings

Once you make a customer or once you establish a referral source member, don't "lov'um and leav'um". Keep in touch with all of them on a *regular monthly basis*. The first thing that you must do is to type up the names, address, city-state-zip on a sheet of paper in a prescribed way so as all the persons in your files can be photocopied onto specially made pressure-sensitive label sheets found at most stationers. You type 33 names and addresses on a sheet of 8 1/2" x 11" typing paper and go to your nearest photocopy place and ask them to photocopy the names onto sheets of pressure- sensitive labels. Later, you will simply peel off the labels and stick them onto monthly greeting cards that you send out to *everyone* in your files. Every month there is some type of holiday or celebration going on. In January there is New Year's, in February there is Valentines Day, in March there is St. Patrick's Day, in April there is Easter. Even in month's like September and August when not much is going on, you can still send them a type of greeting card which says something like "Just a note to say hello". The idea is that you want to stay in the forefront of the mind of *everyone* you have had contact with. Have you ever noticed how big companies like Coca Cola, Chrysler, or Kellogg's spend *millions* on advertisement and billboards just to *stay in the forefront* of your mind. They *know* that sooner or later you are going to be in the mood for drinking a soda, buying a car, or eating some cereal. When that urge hits, they want to be absolutely sure that the soda, car, or cereal you buy is a Coke, Chrysler, or Kellogg's. They know that when you are ready to buy anything the mind will search in it's memory for the *most familiar* products first. Just like Coca Cola, Chrysler, or Kellogg's, you are operating a business also. If you are ever to grow and become a giant in your industry, you must keep your image present in the minds of your contacts, clients, and referral source network. *Start* by sending monthly greetings.

Chapter 19

HOW TO SELL A DECORATION
TO A CLIENT

You know how to decorate. You know where to find and interest prospective clients. Now comes the moment of truth when you are belly-to-belly, toe-to-toe, and eyeball-to-eyeball with your client. You must now sell a decoration and write up a contract. To do this effectively there are certain preliminaries that lay the groundwork and set the stage.

Smile A Lot

Whether you receive your prospective clients in your office or go to theirs - *smile* a lot. It doesn't cost much; it is highly effective, and puts both you and your client at ease.

Dress For Success

You must absolutely and positively dress for success when you are face-to-face with a client. This means a three-piece business suit in the case of a man and a tasteful and color-coordinated business dress for women. If you have trouble in this regard of selecting and knowing how to dress, I suggest that you pick up copies of business magazines such as *Forbes*, *Business Week*, or *Black Enterprise* and notice how the male and female models are dressed in office situations that you find in the color advertising and articles. When you see a picture of a very well-dressed man or woman, study and notice the apparel combinations that make their outfits effective - then go out and imitate the look. Keep "copy-catting" a well-dressed business look whenever you see it, and you will find that, with time, dressing well will soon become second nature to you.

Sell Designs - Not Balloons

You are a balloon *decorator*, a balloon *designer*, and a *balloon artist*, but you are *not* a balloon *vendor*. Never quote your fees by balloon. *Never*! If you offer a client a 6 arch tunnel design over the dance area and if they ask you how many balloons do you use, you *must* say, "Oh, I don't know. We never count balloons. We charge by *design*." Saying this, the *exact* number of balloons will be no longer be of importance. But the minute you say something like "We put 40 balloons per arch; and we charge you $1.00 per balloon", you're finished. They will actually, at some point of the affair, stand in front of your decoration and *count* the balloons on each arch, and woe-be-it to you if one or two balloons happens to be missing. Some people will actually ask for a $1.00 or $2.00 refund. You see, the secret is that you never *really* want your clients to know *how* you come about your prices. For all they know, you may have been handed a mystical invoice from beyond. They must never know how you come about your prices. *You* may know that your charge $1.00 per balloon, but don't let *them* know that you are charging $1.00 per balloon. Another thing that you want to keep in mind is that you must *try to give them as few prices as possible.* If you are charging $250 for six single arches, $25 for a set of King-7, and $175 to do their tables, don't say, "Your six arches are $250, your King-7 set $25, and your tables $175." This is hammering them with too many different prices. You would say something like, "To do your six-arch tunnel, your King-7, and all of your tables would be $450 plus tax."

When you are showing them various designs you must never give any prices until they *ask* for them. It is not until they say, *"How much?"* that they are *truly* interested. And as soon as you give your price - *shut up!* Don't say a word until *they* respond next.

The "Deep Breathers" And The "Scratchers"

They say, *"How much is the weave, King-7, and twenty tables?"* "$450," you say. *Silence.* Your client lets out a deep breath and smiles. Or your client, after hearing the price, *doesn't breathe at all.* What he or she does is *carefully* move one hand and *scratch* the top of the other. They may scratch the side of their cheek or the inside of either leg. Unwittingly this client has *responded.* He or she has just said - "Wow! *That's too much!*" This is body language at it's best. I have observed this reaction many, many times, and I am always fascinated how consistently it occurs. If you don't reassure your client at this point, he or she will now begin to look over their shoulders and make it for the door. They will try to escape by saying that they must check the price over with some other person. Don't believe it. They're just scared. They want to make a quick getaway. So you say to them, "I'm not here to embarrass you, but rather to help you. I realize that everyone is on a budget. Even such large companies as the Holiday or Kentucky Fried Chicken will call and tell me, 'Charles, we need decorations for such-and-such, and we can spend only $250 or $300. What can you do for us?' So, if you would tell me the *most* you can *comfortably* invest in your decoration, I am sure I can design something beautiful and affordable for you." At this point they'll usually sigh with relief and become honest with you. They'll say something like, "Well, we *really* can afford only $250.00 for decorations." You then say, "Fine, let's see what nice designs we have available for your budget." You then proceed to make a sale of $250.00.

Writing Up The Contract

To write up a decoration contract, I suggest that you go to your nearest stationery store and get a book of contract invoices. While writing in the details of what is to be done, ask them how they heard about you. Write the name of your referral source on your client's index file card right above the invoice number. (See illustration, The Index File-Card.) You ask what time their guests arrive and what time the hall is available. Write this in the upper left hand corner of your invoice contract. You need this information to make out your decoration schedule card. Always request a 50% deposit to confirm the decoration with the entire balance payable *before* the day of the event. If you accept personal checks, be sure that there is at least two weeks before the date to allow for it to clear. You want to be a decorator not a collection agency. If you are dealing with someone you know and trust or a very large and well established company, you may accept a 50% deposit and the balance to be paid on the day of the event. But always exercise judgment before you do this.

The type of invoice book that I suggest you utilize is the type that has four copies and carbonless paper. The Rediform company puts out such an invoice book. Most importantly, as a protection against loss to you, get a small rubber stamp made which says "*No refunds available*", and be sure to stamp it on all four copies. This way you'll never have to return a deposit after you've gone to the trouble of booking them in and ordering their supplies. Be sure you have indicated on the contract the total amount of the decoration (plus tax). Subtract the 50% deposit and indicate the balance due and the date due. You *both* sign the agreement, and you give your client the top copy and you keep the other three bottom copies. When they mail in or come in to pay the balance, you mark the remaining three copies paid-in-full and give or send your client the second copy. The third copy can be used as the decoration guide when you go out to decorate, and the fourth copy always remains in your files.

Last but not least, the best way to record all of your decorations for quick and easy reference in addition to your index file cards and invoice book is to write each decoration on a *wall* calendar which is always close to your working area. The type of wall calendar that I suggest shows *all twelve months* of the year *at once*. At a glance you can see *all* of your decoration contracts.

161

Chapter 20

THE LUCRATIVE FUTURE OF THE
BALLOON DECORATION PROFESSION

We now come to the end of our journey through the world of the balloon decorating. Though it be the end of this treatise, it is the beginning of your future.

If we look at the number of balloon companies listed under the *Balloons-Novelty & Toy* classification in all of the current yellow pages throughout the United States, we will find something like 8500 companies. Under the classification of *Florists*, we find that there are currently about 50,000. And both of these yellow pages classifications do not take into account the *thousands* of balloon companies and florists that operate from a *home base*. Why do I mention balloon companies and florists in the same breath? The reason is that balloon companies and florists are *parallel* industries. They both serve exactly the same type of clientele. The same type of person who will order a bouquet of *balloons* is the same type of person who will order a bouquet of *flowers*. Likewise, the same kind of person who will decorate a wedding with flowers is the same person who will decorate a wedding with balloons. This being so, we have a tremendous *need* for more balloon artists. We have immediate openings for at least 41,500 *new* balloon artists in the United States who want to earn $100,000 per year. At this point, in terms of filling this need, we have only a few drops in the barrel. All of the intelligent entrepreneurs and visionaries who realize that this new industry is here to stay and who take action *now* to start their balloon decoration businesses, will be the vanguards and leaders of the future. I predict that it will still be another 5 to 10 years before the balloon decoration profession *begins* to reach it's peak. *Now* is the time. Go for it. I'll see you at the top.

Recommended Reading:

The Silva Mind Control Method For Business Managers by Jose Silva. Pocket Books New York, New York. Paperback $3.95. This book is a must for learning proven scientific method for triggering creative solutions to your toughest problems.

Power Selling By Telephone by Barry Z. Masser & William M. Leeds. Parker Publishing Co. Paperback. West, Nyack, New York 10994

"Souvenir" magazine published by Talcott Communications Corporation, 1414 Merchandise Mart, Chicago, IL, 60654, (312) 670-0800. Charles Prosper writes a balloon art column each issue. It comes out six times a year and costs $18.00 to subscribe.

"Flower &" magazine is the principal monthly floral magazine which does special features on balloons and balloon artistry five times a year in the February, June, August, October, and December issues. This magazine is published by Telefora Plaza, Suite 260, 12233 W. Olympic Blvd., Los Angeles, California 90064, (213) 826-5253. Yearly subscription is $24.00.

Appendix:

For more information about out schedule of seminars given around the country as well as our mail order catalogue of books, cassettes, video, and wholesale decorating items, please call or write:

Global Publishing Company
Post Office Box 35357
Los Angeles, CA 90035
(213) 937-4356

PHOTO ORDER FORM

Global Publishing Company
Post Office Box 35357
Los Angeles, CA 90035
(213) 937-4356

Please send me the following 8" x 10" color photos of the following designs at $15.00 each. If I order ten photos or more I pay only $12.00 each, and if I order twenty photos or more I pay only $10.00 each. Thanks.

Description	#Photos	Code	Amount
1. 6 Single Arch Rainbow Tunnel (Bold Colors)		A-1	
2. 6 Single Arch Rainbow Tunnel (Pastel Colors)		A-2	
3. 1 Weave and King-7 (Pink and Pearl)		A-3	
4. 1 Sectional Rainbow Weave (Bold Colors)		A-4	
5. 6 Single Arch Tunnel (Pink,Clear,and Pearl)		A-5	
6. 1 Floating Number "13" (Lilac,Pink,White)		A-6	
7. 1 Floating Heart (Pink and White)		A-7	
8. 1 Pair of Rainbow Clowns (Bold)		A-8	
9. 1 Pair of Rainbow Clowns (Pastel)		A-9	
10. 1 Pair of Snowmen With Balloon Christmas Wreath		A-10	
11. 1 Pair of Snowmen With Balloon Poinsettias		A-11	
12. The Bride & Groom With Pink & Pearl Balloon Flowers		A-12	
13. The Tuxedo Men		A-13	
14. The Balloon Fruit		A-14	
15. The Candle & Bow Centerpiece (Lilac & White)		A-15	
16. The Chamay & Bow Centerpiece (Pink & White)		A-16	
17. The Chamay & Bow Centerpiece (Pale Blue & White)		A-17	
18. The Swan & Bow Centerpiece (Pink & White)		A-18	
19. The Plush White Poodle Arrangement (Red Bow)		A-19	
20. The Plush Brown Teddy Bear Arrangement (Pink Bow)		A-20	
21. The Plush White Teddy Bear & Chamay Arrangement (Red Bow)		A-21	
22. The Plush Brown Teddy Bear & Jelly Bean Arrangement (Red Bow)		A-22	
23. 1 Set of 3 King-7 (Pink & Pearl)		A-23	

Name:_____

Address:_____

City:_____ State:_____ Zip:_____

Californians: Please add 7% sales tax.

(You may send photocopies of this order form.)

BOOK ORDER FORM

Global Publishing Company
Post Office Box 35357
Los Angeles, CA 90035
(213) 937-4356

Please send me:

_____ **How To Become A Balloon Artist**
copies **And Make Up To $100,000 A Year @ $35.00 each**

I understand that I may return this book for a full refund within a 30 day trial period if I am not 100% satisfied.

Name:_____

Address:_____

City:_____State:_____Zip:_____

Californians: Please add $2.45 (7% sales tax)
Shipping: $1 for the first book and $.50 for each additional book.

_____ I can't wait 3-4 weeks for Book Rate. Here is $3.00 per book for Air Mail.

_____ Please send me a FREE catalogue of your 8" x 10" color glossy photos available for purchase.

(You may send photocopies of this order form.)